Fonzie Drops In!

"It's not all it's cracked up to be," Fonzie said.

"What?"

"Being out of school."

"You could go back," Richie suggested.

"I was thinking about it," Fonzie said. "But I guess it's too late. I've been out a whole year."

"What's a year?" Richie said. "If you wanted to, you could do it."

"Yeah, if I *wanted* to, I guess I could. You're right—what's a year?" He began crumpling up the paper. "You want to know something? I've been thinking about it for a couple days or so . . . just thinking. It was always a lot of fun . . . some of it . . ."

"Yeah, there's dances, basketball, football, pep rallies."

Fonzie winced. "That's kid stuff. I'm talking about real fun. Like when you show a girl your tattoo behind the gym."

Richie grinned. "Why don't you come on back, Fonzie?"

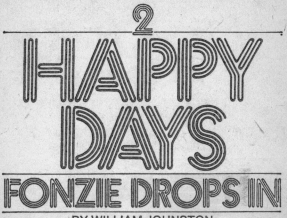

2 HAPPY DAYS
FONZIE DROPS IN

BY WILLIAM JOHNSTON

tempo
books

GROSSET & DUNLAP
PUBLISHERS · NEW YORK

ISBN: 0-448-07452-6

A Tempo Books Original
Tempo Books is registered in the U.S. Patent Office

Printed in the United States of America

ONE

It was noon. The September weather was still warm enough for the high school kids to eat lunch out-of-doors. On an outside basketball court, a half-dozen boys were playing a ragged game of three-on-three. One of the boys was Richie Cunningham. He was lean and quick but not especially serious about the game. Another was Ralph, a close friend of Richie's. Ralph was big-boned and redheaded.

Watching the boys was a trio of girls, Trudy, Sandy and Alice. They were seated cross-legged on the grass, munching on sandwiches and sipping from containers of milk. When a basket was made—which was not often—they responded in unison with cheers. Their interest in the subtleties of the game—dribbling, faking, passing off—however, was minimal.

The other spectator, Fonzie, was wholly oblivious to the action on the basketball court. Fonzie, dark-eyed and sharp-featured, was also seated on the grass. He was hunched forward slightly, his attention fixed on the current issue of *Hot Rod* magazine, which was open in front of him. School-connected activities—even a pickup basketball game—held little attraction for Fonzie. He was a drop-out.

On the court, an opposition player drove toward the basket, which was being guarded by

Ralph. Abruptly, he halted, performed a full turn, then went up for the shot. Ralph went up with him and tipped the ball away, blocking the shot. The ball bounced free. Richie scooped it in, took it out, then fired it to Ralph. Ralph went up once more, this time with the ball. It was an easy lay-up. The ball dropped through the net.

The girls cheered.

But the boy who had had the ball originally claimed a foul.

"You hacked me!" he said indignantly to Ralph.

"I didn't hack you," Ralph replied disgustedly. "How did I hack you? I didn't even touch you."

"You hacked me!" the boy insisted.

"I didn't see it," Richie said.

"I didn't hack him," Ralph said. "I'd know it if I did, wouldn't I?" He called over to Fonzie. "Hey, Fonzie! Did I hack him?"

Without looking up, Fonzie responded with a thumbs down signal. "No hack."

The boy who had claimed the foul shrugged resignedly. "Okay. What's the score?"

"Even. Fourteen-fourteen," Richie said.

"What wins it—two?" another player asked.

"Two baskets," Richie replied.

At that moment, Potsie, another close friend of Richie's came trotting up. He was carrying a school book. Potsie was a lot like Ralph in size. But he had a somewhat more exuberant, aggressive manner.

"Hey, need another guy?" Potsie said.

"We already got sides," Richie told him.

"Aw. . . ." Potsie suddenly brightened. "Hey, Rich, I got my history exam back."

"Come on, Rich, let's go," an opposition player said, bouncing the ball.

"Okay, just a second," Richie addressed Potsie again. "What did you get?"

Now, Ralph complained, "Come on, Richie, are we playing or not?"

"Did you pass?" Richie asked Potsie.

"I don't know. Probably not. I'm afraid to look."

"You mean you got your paper back and you don't even know what you got on it?"

Potsie took a paper from the book. "You look," he said.

Richie accepted the exam paper from him and opened it and immediately broke into a grin. "It's a B-plus," he said.

Excited, Potsie snatched the paper back. "Let me see!"

"Rich, will you come on?" another player called. "The bell's going to ring in a minute."

"B-plus!" Potsie said, amazed. Then, recovering, he shrugged indifferently. "I knew I had it cinched," he said, wadding the paper into a ball. "It was a breeze."

From the school building came the sound of the bell that ended the lunch period.

"Cripes! I knew it!" the boy with the ball said.

"Well, back to the salt mines," Ralph said.

The girls began rising, collecting sandwich wrappings and empty milk containers.

"How about after school? Want to finish the game then?" the boy with the ball asked Richie.

"I don't know."

"Not me," another boy said. "I got to stay after."

Potsie tossed the wadded up test paper toward a trash basket. It missed and landed near Fonzie, who raised his eyes from *Hot Rod* magazine and glared at it.

"Let's go," Potsie said to the others.

"What's your hurry?"

"I got biology," Potsie replied. "We're going to cut up a frog."

Trudy made a face. "Ugh! Right after lunch?"

Potsie grinned. "Yeah, I never thought of that."

"I bet somebody'll throw up," the boy with the ball said.

Sandy tried to change the subject. "I have French," she said.

"Ooo-la-la," Ralph said, grinning. "I'll walk you."

They began straggling off. After they had gone a short distance, Richie glanced back and saw that Fonzie had picked up Potsie's discarded test paper and was studying it. Fonzie's expression was uncharacteristically intent. Still looking back, Richie fell behind the group. Fonzie was now talking to himself. Curious, Richie returned.

"Hey, Fonzie, don't you have to get back to work?" he said.

"I'm taking the afternoon off." Fonzie's eyes were still on the test paper.

"Something up?" Richie asked.

"Nah. I'll probably go park behind the drive-in and practice spitting through my teeth."

"Oh . . . That's nice."

"What about you?" Fonzie, asked, finally raising his eyes from the paper. "Don't you have to go to class?"

Richie shook his head. "I've got a free period."

"Want to come down to Arnold's and practice with me?"

"Naw. I . . . uh . . . I'm not much at spitting."

"You know, I know all these answers," Fonzie said, indicating the test paper.

"Yeah?"

"Sure." Fonzie began reading. "The Senate . . . the House of Representatives . . . the Supreme Court. . ." He looked up again. "I know all that stuff."

"Great."

"What were the questions, though?" Fonzie said.

Richie frowned, thinking. "I don't know. I forget."

"It doesn't make any difference," Fonzie said. "If you know the answers, who cares if you know the questions or not, right?"

"Well. . . ." Richie sat down beside him. "Hey, Fonz, do you ever wish you hadn't dropped out of school?"

"Nah. Too many rules," Fonzie replied.

"I guess it doesn't matter," Richie said. "You're doing all right as a mechanic."

"All right? I'm doing great."

"Yeah, great. You're kind of the Mickey Mantle of the grease pit," Richie said.

"I'm the best," Fonzie agreed.

"Yeah, I know." Richie looked at him admiringly. "I bet it's neat being in the adult world," he said.

Fonzie shrugged. "Nothing's perfect."

"What do you mean?"

"Everybody's married," Fonzie said. "They all go home after work. All except Old Roscoe, the lube man."

"Is he your friend?"

"He's seventy years old," Fonzie said.

Richie thought about it for a moment. "That's *too* adult," he decided.

"We go out for beers after work," Fonzie told him.

"That's okay."

"That's dull," Fonzie said. "All he talks about is his truss. I know that truss like it was my own. If I ever decide to give up mechanics, I could go around the country giving lectures on Old Roscoe's truss."

Richie laughed.

"It's not all it's cracked up to be," Fonzie said.

"What?"

"Being out of school."

"You could go back," Richie suggested.

Fonzie looked at the test paper again. "I was thinking about it," he said. "But I guess it's too late. I've been out a whole year."

"What's a year?" Richie said. "If you wanted to, you could do it."

"Yeah, if I *wanted* to, I guess I could. You're right—what's a year?" He began crumpling up the paper. "You want to know something? I've been thinking about it for a couple days or so . . . just thinking. . . . It was always a lot of fun . . . some of it. . . ."

"Yeah, there's dances, basketball, football, pep rallies."

Fonzie winced. "That's kid stuff. I'm talking about real fun. Like when you show a girl your tattoo behind the gym."

Richie grinned. "Why don't you come on back, Fonzie?"

"Well. . . ."

"There's a whole new crop of girls who haven't seen your tattoo," Richie said.

"Yeah. . . ."

"Hey, you know, you'd be kind of a celebrity."

Fonzie looked at him doubtfully. "My tattoo ain't that great."

"No, I mean you'd be the only high school drop-in," Richie said. "A lot of guys drop out, but how many drop in? You'd be one of a kind."

"That's right. I'd be kind of like a war hero."

Richie frowned. "What's the connection?"

"Coming back," Fonzie explained. "It'd be like I've been off to the war, and now I'm back. Cool." He began rising. "I think I'll go up to the Principal's office right now and tell them." He hesitated. "How do you think they'll take it?"

"Great," Richie replied, getting up. "Why wouldn't they?"

"You're right. I'm like a lost sheep and they're getting me back in the flock."

"Let me know what happens," Richie said.

"I'll do better than that," Fonzie told him. "I'm taking you with me. You can *see* what happens."

"Are you sure you want me along?" Richie said. "It's kind of personal."

"I might need you for a reference," Fonzie said. He gave Richie a gentle shove in the direction of the school building. "Let's get it over with."

The second bell rang, announcing that classes had started.

"What about your job?" Richie asked Fonzie. "Are you just going to quit?"

"I dropped out of school, didn't I? Why can't I drop out of work?"

"I was just thinking, though, it's a good job, and you like it."

"Yeah, I like it. No girls, though."

"School isn't all girls, either, Fonzie, remember."

"It was before," Fonzie said. "Has it changed that much?"

"I guess it *is* all girls, if that's the way you look at it," Richie said. "But maybe that's why—"

Fonzie interrupted. "Hey, listen, are you trying to talk me out of this?"

"No, only—"

"Okay, then," Fonzie said, breaking in again. "Either you're for me or you're against me. If you're for me, say anything you want. If you're against me, shut up."

"Got it," Richie said.

They entered the school building and walked along the vacated corridor toward the main office.

"Good old halls," Fonzie said sentimentally. "They're just the same—empty."

"They're not usually empty."

"They were empty a lot for me," Fonzie said. "When I skipped classes I used to sneak out when nobody was around."

"You're not going to do that again, though, are you?" Richie said.

"Nah. I don't do kid stuff like that any more. If I want to skip classes, I'll walk out whether anybody's watching or not."

"Fonzie, what I mean is—"

"Hey, here we are!"

They entered the office and approached the desk, where Miss Marble, the principal's secretary, a plump, motherly, gray-haired woman, was putting attendance forms in order.

"Could we see Mr. Faraday?" Richie asked.

Miss Marble raised her eyes from the forms. She smiled at Richie, then, becoming aware of Fonzie, flinched.

"Long time no see," Fonzie said to her.

"Suddenly, it doesn't seem so long," Miss Marble replied. She returned her attention to Richie. "What about, dear?" she asked.

"It's kind of private."

"I'm coming back to school," Fonzie told her.

She stared at him. "What have we done to you?"

"No, Fonzie is turning over a new leaf, sort of," Richie said.

"Uh-huh," Miss Marble said dubiously. "Well . . . I'll see if Mr. Faraday is free."

She left the desk and went into the Principal's office.

"What's she got against you?" Richie asked Fonzie.

"She always used to call me by my name, Arthur, and I never knew who she was talking to, so I didn't answer," Fonzie explained.

"Oh."

Miss Marble returned. "He'll see you," she said.

Richie and Fonzie entered the office. Mr. Faraday, tall and white-haired and distinguished-looking, was seated at his desk. He peered warily at the boys over the rims of his wire frame spectacles. Then, relaxing his manner a bit, he motioned to chairs.

"So, Arthur," the Principal said, as Richie and Fonzie sat down facing him, "Miss Marble tells me you want to come back to school."

"Right," Fonzie replied briskly.

"May I ask why?"

"Sure," Fonzie answered.

Mr. Faraday waited.

Fonzie stared at him noncommittally.

"Well, *why do you* want to return?" Mr. Faraday asked.

Fonzie deferred to Richie. "Tell him," he said.

"Oh!" Richie said, caught off guard. "Well . . . uh . . . he. . . . Uh, well, sir, it's this way—" He spoke quickly to Fonzie, keeping his voice down. "The tattoo?"

Fonzie grimaced, shaking his head.

"Actually," Richie said, facing the Principal again, "it's, uh, well, Fonzie feels that there's a cultural void in his life . . . kind of. . . ."

Fonzie brightened. "Hey, that's good."

Encouraged, Richie continued. "He's been thinking," he told the Principal, "and he realizes that there's more to life than just having a job. So, what he wants to do is finish his education so he can pursue a more satisfying profession."

"Good, very good," Fonzie said, nodding agreement.

"Does Arthur understand that he will be expected to conform to the rules?" Mr. Faraday asked Richie.

"Oh, sure."

"Very well. You can tell Arthur that he can start in the morning."

Richie turned to Fonzie to pass on the message. But Fonzie raised a hand, stopping him. Then, rising, he extended the hand toward the Principal.

"Cool," Fonzie said.

The Principal took the hand. "Yes . . ."

"Let's blow," Fonzie said to Richie, retrieving his hand.

"Oh, Arthur, just a minute," Mr. Faraday said. "I was wondering if you might have a minute to look at my car. I'm having trouble with the clutch again. It's slipping."

"I told you, you've got to stop driving with your foot on the clutch," Fonzie said.

"Yes, I know, you told me, but—"

"You don't listen," Fonzie said.

"I'm sorry. But if you could just look at it—"

Fonzie shook his head. "I won't touch that clutch again until you promise you won't drive with your foot on it. It's a waste of time. I fix it, you goof it up. What's the point? See what I mean?"

"Yes, but—I won't do it again."

"Sure, you say it, but how do I know I can believe it?"

"Honest, Arthur, I—"

"I want to hear a promise."

Mr. Faraday sighed. "All right. I promise."

"You promise what?"

"I promise I won't drive with my foot on the clutch again."

"This is your last chance," Fonzie told him.

"I understand."

"Okay," Fonzie said. "Bring it around to the shop tomorrow after school."

The Principal beamed. "Thank you, Arthur. Thank you very much."

"Just don't forget, you're on thin ice with that clutch," Fonzie said, as he and Richie backed out of the office. "Once more, after I fix it, and you can get yourself another mechanic."

"I know. Don't worry. A promise is a promise."

When Richie and Fonzie reached the outer office, Fonzie paused at the desk.

"It's all set," he told Miss Marble. "I start tomorrow."

"I'll make out your schedule," she said drearily.

"Which classes do you plan to skip? I'll just leave those off and save myself a lot of bother."

"What's that stuff with numbers?"

"Math?"

"Math?"

"That's it," Fonzie said. "Scratch math."

Miss Marble nodded bleakly.

Richie and Fonzie departed and walked toward the exit.

"If you're going to work on Mr. Faraday's car, I guess you're going to keep your job, too," Richie said.

"It won't hurt to keep my hand in," Fonzie said. "I can work at the shop after school."

"That'll be kind of a tough schedule," Richie said.

"Nah," Fonzie said. "School'll be a breeze. I already know the answers. The Senate . . . the House of Representatives . . . the Supreme Court. . . ."

TWO

The confusion that was referred to as "breakfast time" was in progress in the Cunningham kitchen. The mother, Marion, was at a counter, dicing cucumber slices on a cutting board. Howard, the father, having finished his morning meal, was standing near the table, holding the paper open in front of him, hoping to finish reading it before he left for work. The daughter, Joanie, younger than Richie, was about to duck under the paper to get to the table with two slices of buttered toast.

"I'll have your lunch ready in just a second, dear," Marion told her husband.

"What's that?" Howard said, as an oily splotch began to appear in the spot where he had been reading.

"I said your lunch is almost ready."

"I know what you said, Marion. I'm asking what this blob is on my paper."

"Oh . . . butter, I guess," Joanie informed him. "I think I brushed the paper when I went under."

"You could at least have left some jelly, too," her father said. "You know I like butter and jelly on my paper."

"No, dear, I'm giving you beef sandwich spread with diced cucumbers," Marion said. "You had peanut butter and jelly yesterday."

14

"Marion, I didn't— Beef sandwich spread with diced cucumbers?"

"Yes. It's one of your favorites," Marion replied, packing the sandwiches into a brown paper bag.

Howard and Joanie exchanged looks, then Howard quickly folded the paper and headed for the door.

Marion turned from the counter as he was going by and put the brown paper bag into his hand.

"Oh-oh—you almost forgot your lunch," she said.

"Oh . . . yes . . . ." He kissed his wife on the cheek. "Goodbye, dear . . . ."

"Goodbye, Howard. What's the weather?"

"I don't need my rubbers."

"All right, dear." Marion turned back to the counter.

"I'll just leave the paper here on the table," Howard said, putting down the brown paper bag instead. " 'Bye all—see you tonight." He hurried from the kitchen.

"Where is Richie?" Marion asked Joanie.

"Looking at himself in the bathroom mirror the last time I saw him."

"He's going to be late." She went to the kitchen doorway and called toward the front stairs. "Richeeeeeee!"

Richie answered from upstairs. "I'm coming, Mom."

Starting back toward the counter, Marion saw the brown paper bag on the table. "Oh, my heavens, your father is getting absent-minded," she said to Joanie. "Look. He left his lunch and took the paper."

"He didn't exactly forget his lunch, Mother."

"What do you mean?"

"He left it on purpose," Joanie told her. "He says a beef sandwich spread with diced cucumbers is ookie."

Marion's eyebrows arched. "I never knew that."

"He didn't tell you because he didn't want to hurt your feelings."

"Oh, I'm sure you're wrong. I've always thought a beef sandwich spread with diced cucumbers was one of his favorites."

Richie arrived. "Hi!" he said amiably.

"Richie," Marion said, "did you know that your father thinks a beef sandwich spread with diced cucumbers is ookie?"

"Sure," he replied, sitting down at the table.

"Well, the wife is always the last to know," Marion said, going on to the counter. "I wonder what else your father doesn't like. Maybe I should change my perfume."

"If you're wearing beef sandwich spread with diced cucumbers, you better," Joanie said. "Try peanut butter and jelly."

"Hey, Mom," Richie said, "know what I did? I talked my friend Fonzie into going back to school."

"Very good, Richard. A boy needs a good education to get by today. Fonzie? Isn't that your friend who rides a motorcycle?"

"Yeah. He's a great mechanic, too." He gulped

down his orange juice. "Got to go," he said, rising. "This is Fonzie's first day back at school."

"Richard! You haven't had breakfast!"

"I'll bum a jellyroll off Potsie," he told her, ducking out.

"That'll be good for a few cavities," Marion said to Joanie.

"I have to get to school early, too," Joanie said, rising.

"Why? Are they having some sort of Welcome Home celebration for Fonzie?"

"No, not that."

"Then why?"

"Jean Marie Scarsdale is going to tell us where babies come from," Joanie replied. "She's got a book—with pictures and everything."

Marion turned to her. "You sit right down," she said sharply. "I'll drive you to school. We'll have a little talk on the way."

"Okay," Joanie replied, sinking back into her chair. "But it won't be the same without pictures."

"I managed to have all of my children without seeing any pictures," Marion told her. "Frankly, it's one of those things where, if you have to have a picture drawn for you, you might as well forget it. Get your books," she said, leaving the counter. "I'll go out and warm up the car."

"Why do you always have to warm up the car?" Joanie asked.

"I haven't the faintest idea. Your father told me to, that's all I know," Marion replied. "I suppose it's because cars are just like everybody else, it takes them a while to get their blood circulating in the morning. Hurry, now!"

Arriving at Jefferson High School, Richie met Potsie and Ralph at the usual place, on the steps. They took up their accustomed position, just to the right of the doors, where they could see everything that was going on without impeding traffic. Potsie opened the brown paper bag he was carrying. Richie reached in and pulled out a jellyroll.

"Where is he?" Ralph said.

"He'll be here," Richie replied. But he did not sound at all certain.

"What does a great mechanic want to come back to school for?" Potsie asked.

"With more schooling he could become an engineer," Richie said.

"He doesn't even *like* trains."

The first bell sounded.

"We better go," Ralph said. "He's not coming."

"Will you just give it a minute?" Richie said crossly.

"Look, Richie, it's not your fault if he doesn't show up," Potsie said.

"He'll be here, I tell you."

"I'm not going to be late for class," Ralph said.

"Okay, you guys go ahead," Richie said. "I'm just going to wait another couple seconds."

Ralph and Potsie joined the other students who were entering the building. Still, Richie lingered. When, finally, he was the only one left on the steps, he turned toward the doors, disappointed. At that same instant, he heard the roar of a motorcycle. Looking back, he saw Fonzie ride up.

"You're late!" Richie called out.

"I'm not late," Fonzie replied. "All you eager beavers are early."

"See you!" Richie called.

"Right!"

Richie hurried into the building, then paused for a look back. Fonzie was swaggering toward the entrance. Grinning, Richie ran on.

Mrs. Wimper, the history teacher, was writing on the board when Richie reached the classroom. He got to his seat just as the second bell rang.

"He's here," Richie whispered to Ralph.

"I told you he'd show up," Ralph replied. "What were you worried about?"

"Where is he?" Potsie whispered to Richie.

"Getting his schedule, probably."

"Do you think—"

Mrs. Wimper, having turned from the blackboard, interrupted the conversation by rapping on her desk with a ruler.

"All right, class . . . if we can just settle down now. . . ," Mrs. Wimper said.

The murmuring continued.

"Class . . . put your books under your desks and get out a sheet of paper. We're going to have a pop quiz."

"Oh, boy, a quiz about our fathers," Potsie said.

There were groans.

Mrs. Wimper, a stout woman, who wore a pince-nez pinned to the bosom of her dress, raised the glasses and peered icily at Potsie. "We can do nicely without that," she informed him.

Potsie pulled his head in.

"I hope you have all studied Chapter Sixteen," Mrs. Wimper went on. "Because today—"

The classroom door had opened. Fonzie entered.

"May I help you, sir?" Mrs. Wimper asked.

"I ain't a sir," Fonzie replied. "I'm a new kid."

"You're—" She seemed unwilling to accept the idea.

Fonzie handed her his admission slip.

"Hey, Fonz!" Ralph called out, waving.

Fonzie winked.

The murmuring began again, as the students leaned across the aisles, to get a better look at him.

Mrs. Wimper rapped on the desk with the ruler again. "Class! Quiet, please!" She indicated Fonzie. "We have a new student with us. This is Arthur Fonzarelli."

There were cheers.

"You seem to be very popular," Mrs. Wimper said to Fonzie.

"What can you do?" Fonzie replied. "When you got it, you got it." He frowned. "By the way, that Arthur Fonzarelli business, you can skip that," he told Mrs. Wimper. "I like to be called Fonzie."

"Oh. Well. . . . All right, you may take a seat . . . uh . . . Fonzie. . . ."

Fonzie shuffled along an aisle until he reached the seat that was across from Richie's. It was occupied by a freckled-faced, red-haired boy with a crewcut.

"I think I would enjoy sitting there," he said.

Quickly, the redheaded boy got his books from under the seat and moved.

Fonzie started to settle in the seat. But as he was sitting down, his attention was caught by an especially pretty girl, a blond, a short distance away. Immediately, he straightened. For a second, Fonzie seemed undecided. Then his expression showed clearly that the solution to the dilemma had come to him.

"You, up," he said to the boy on the other side of him.

Puzzledly, the boy got his books and stood.

Fonzie next addressed the blond. "You, here," he said to her, indicating the seat that the boy had vacated. And, when she had moved, Fonzie spoke once more to the boy. "You, there," he commanded, pointing to the seat that the girl had left. The boy obeyed.

"Now, students—" Mrs. Wimper began.

But Fonzie hadn't finished. He had the boy who was seated behind him on his feet and was directing a dark-haired girl to the desk.

"Fonzie—" Mrs. Wimper said.

"Be with you in a minute."

Fonzie motioned to the boy in front of him. When the boy rose, Fonzie signaled to another blond girl. She moved to the boy's desk and he sat down in the seat that she had previously occupied.

Fonzie surveyed the new arrangement. He now

had a pretty girl in front of him, to his right, behind him, and Richie to his left. He appeared pleased.

"Fonzie, you're disrupting the class," Mrs. Wimper said.

"I was just doing a little shifting," Fonzie said, sitting down. "I need the right atmosphere, you know."

"But I had everybody seated in alphabetical order to match my seating plan," Mrs. Wimper protested.

Fonzie was apologetic. "Hey, I'm sorry. I didn't know. But, if you don't know somebody's name, just ask me." He leaned forward and addressed the blond he had seated in front of him. "Hey, what's your name?"

She turned, blessing him with a smile of fascination and admiration. "Polly Wilson," she told him.

"I had to know in case the teach asked," Fonzie said.

"I think it's just *won*derful what you're doing," Polly said.

Fonzie shrugged. "Anybody can move people around in their seats."

"No, I mean coming back to school. It shows such—"

"Students! Please!" Mrs. Wimper said, her patience finally exhausted.

The blond faced front.

"As I was saying," Mrs. Wimper began, speaking to the class. Pausing, she closed her eyes for a moment. "What *was* I saying?" she murmured.

"Canceling the quiz?" Potsie suggested.

She ignored the remark. "Chapter Sixteen," she said, opening her eyes. "Before we begin, I want to emphasize one important contribution to domestic stability made by President Truman."

"Yeah, he got everybody to take piano lessons," Ralph said.

Snickers.

"And he added a few new 'words' to the dictionary," Potsie said.

There was a burst of laughter.

"Students!" Mrs. Wimper said crossly.

But the burst of laughter had set off a chain reaction of whispers and giggles.

Then Fonzie rose. "Cool it," he said, glowering.

There was instant quiet.

Fonzie, sitting down, motioned to Mrs. Wimper, letting her know that she could now continue.

"Why . . . thank you, Fonzie. . . ."

"It's nothing."

Mrs. Wimper faced the class again. "President Truman—" she said.

She was interrupted this time by the bell that ended the class.

"Dismissed," Mrs. Wimper said feebly.

The students began rising and departing noisily. But Polly Wilson, the blond whom Fonzie had seated in front of him, lingered.

"What I was going to say was," she told Fonzie, blessing him with the adoring smile again, "I think it's just wonderful about your ambition. How many boys are like that?"

"Six, seven?" Fonzie guessed.

"One in a million," she told him. "You're really marvelous."

"I do okay," Fonzie admitted. "If I could just get a little more distance spitting through my teeth, I guess I'd have it made."

Polly Wilson giggled. "And such a delightful sense of humor!" she said.

Then she hurried away.

Fonzie joined Richie and Potsie and they left the classroom together.

"Boy, talk about taking over," Potsie said to Fonzie. "You got Mrs. Wimper *and* Polly Wilson eating right out of your hand."

"Is that good?" Fonzie asked.

"Good? One of the toughest teachers in the whole school *and* Polly Wilson!"

"Who's Polly Wilson?" Fonzie asked, as they reached the corridor.

"The blond."

"I know who she is, I mean who is she?" Fonzie said.

"The head cheerleader," Potsie told him. "The queen."

Fonzie turned to Richie. "The queen?"

"The girl all the other girls are jealous of," Richie explained. "You can tell because anytime you mention her name to any of the other girls, they tell you they're not jealous of her."

Fonzie nodded. "The queen," he said. "Well, it's nothing more than I deserve." He turned to Potsie. "You think she's really gone on me, huh?"

"She talked to you," Potsie said. "That's a dead

give-away. The only other guy she talks to is Freeman Locke, the guy she goes with."

"What do you mean?" Richie said to Potsie. "She talks to other guys."

Potsie shook his head. "She talks 'at' or 'around' other guys," he said. "But Fonzie, she looked him right in the eyes when she talked to him. She really saw him. She talks to Freeman like that, too. Nobody else, though."

"Who's this Freeman Locke?" Fonzie asked.

"A guy," Potsie told him.

"Come on," Richie said. "We got to get to class. Fonzie, what have you got?"

"Algebra."

"I thought you weren't going to take math."

"I got doublecrossed." Fonzie said. "Who's Freeman Locke?"

A bell rang.

"We're late!" Richie said, hurrying off.

"See you," Potsie said to Fonzie, going in the other direction.

"Who's Freeman Locke!" Fonzie shouted after Potsie.

"The math king!"

"Kings . . . queens . . . what ever happened to good old-fashioned democracy?" Fonzie muttered, trudging off toward his next class.

THREE

The after-school crowd was gathering at Arnold's. The juke box had been fed and was responding to the nourishment with Chuck Berry's "Johnny B. Goode." Several couples were already dancing. Others were taking over the booths. Orders for burgers and cokes were being shouted.

One booth was occupied solely by Fonzie. His school books were stacked on the table. But his attention was on *Hot Rod* magazine, which he had open in front of him.

Ralph appeared. "Hey, Fonzie. . . ," he said.

Keeping his eyes on the magazine, Fonzie raised a finger.

"How'd the rest of the day go?" Ralph asked.

"Breeze," Fonzie replied, still not looking up.

"You know, I been wondering. How come you came back to the old brain factory, anyway?"

"I figured the joint could use a little class," Fonzie told him.

Trudy, the dark-haired girl whom Fonzie had seated behind him in history class, appeared. In one hand she had an autograph book.

"Fonzie, it sure is neat having you in school," she said dreamily.

At last, Fonzie raised his eyes from the magazine.

"You're the coolest person we've ever had at Jefferson," Trudy told him. She opened the auto-

26

graph book and flattened it on the table. "Would you?" she asked, offering him a pencil.

"Why not?" Fonzie replied.

"I've got an empty page here between Sal Mineo and Little Anthony," Trudy said.

With a flourish, Fonzie put his name on the page.

"Thanks a bunch!" Trudy said excitedly.

"Any time."

Trudy hurried off to show her new treasure to her friends.

"Cool. Really cool," Ralph said.

"You learn to live with it," Fonzie said.

Richie arrived.

"See you around, Ralph," Fonzie said, dismissing him.

"Oh . . . yeah, right."

When Ralph had gone, Fonzie motioned to Richie. "Park it," he said.

Richie slid into the booth. "How was algebra?" he asked.

"Glad you brought that up," Fonzie said. He closed the magazine and placed it on top of the stack of books. "You know, Richie," he said, "you're a pretty bright guy . . . for a guy who don't ride a motorcycle."

"Thanks."

"You know, this going back to school, it was your idea."

"But you said you were already thinking about it."

"I think about a lot of things," Fonzie said. "I *think* about spitting through my teeth all the way across the Grand Canyon—but I don't *do* anything about it."

Richie nodded. "I see what you mean."

"So, going back to school, it was your idea—right?"

"Right."

"And you want me to do good—right?"

"Uhhh, yeah, right," Richie replied.

"Well, I'm having kind of a tough time getting back in the swing of things," Fonzie said.

"It's only the first day."

"Richie, I think I know if I'm having a tough time getting back in the swing of things or not."

"Sure. Who'd know better than you."

"So, I need your help with homework," Fonzie told him.

"Oh. Okay."

Potsie appeared.

"Hey, Potsie," Richie said.

"What's new?" Potsie asked.

"We're having a private conversation," Fonzie told him.

"What about?"

Fonzie stared at him coldly.

"Oh ... I guess if it's private, then you don't want to tell me what it's about," Potsie said.

"I like a guy who knows when he's butting in," Fonzie said.

"See you," Potsie said to Richie. Then he moved on.

"Now ..." Fonzie said, taking a fold of papers from one of the school books. "... about this X equals Y equals Z stuff. . . ."

"Algebra."

"That's what they call it." Fonzie handed the papers to Richie. "There you go."

"What kind of help do you need?" Richie asked.

"You do it for me," Fonzie said.

"Do it? Do your homework for you? All of it?"

"Not all of it, just the algebra. I'll get somebody else to do the other stuff."

"But, Fonzie, if I do it, how is that going to help you?"

"What's so hard to understand about that?" Fonzie asked. "If you do it, I won't have to. Isn't that help?"

"But you won't know the answers," Richie said.

"Richie, when you get your report card, what does it say on it?" Fonzie replied. "Does it say you know the answers? Or does it say what grade you got, good or bad?"

"It says the grade."

"Do you get a good grade in algebra?"

Richie nodded.

"Okay. If you do my work for me, will I get a good grade in Algebra?"

"I guess so, but—"

"No buts," Fonzie said.

"I don't think you get the idea, though," Richie said. "You see, the point is—"

But he had lost Fonzie's attention. Fonzie was looking across the room, where Polly Wilson and Freeman Locke were taking over a booth that had just been vacated.

"Where did I see him before?" Fonzie asked, indicating the freckled-faced, red-haired boy.

"You changed his seat for him today in history," Richie replied.

"Is that—"

"Freeman Locke."

"That's a king?" Fonzie said.

"He's a math whiz," Richie told him.

Fonzie looked at the fold of papers he had given to Richie. He frowned thoughtfully, then shook his head. "No, you do it for me," he said. "I like to give my business to my friends."

"About that—" Richie said.

Fonzie was rising. "And, listen, don't smudge up the paper," he said. "Maybe neatness counts."

"Fonzie—"

Fonzie was on his way to the other booth.

"Didn't we meet before somewhere?" Fonzie said, easing into the booth beside Polly Wilson. "Where was it, the Riviera? Or Mrs. Wimper's history class? I always get those two places mixed up."

Polly giggled. "Fonzie!"

"Hi, fella," Freeman Locke said.

Fonzie studied him interestedly. "Let me hear you say something in math," he said.

"Hypotenuse," Freeman replied.

"What's it mean?"

"The side of a right triangle opposite the right angle."

Fonzie shrugged. "Could be," he said. "It's all

Greek to me." He turned to Polly again. "Let's talk about me," he said.

"I was just doing that," she said. "I was telling Freeman. You could be a legend."

"Could be?" Fonzie said. "I thought I already was."

"I mean seriously," Polly said. "Can't you just see the movie? You're a mechanic, working in a dirty old garage, and suddenly, you're inspired. You go back to school, and then the next thing anybody knows, you're a captain in industry."

"What'd I do, marry the boss's daughter?" Fonzie asked.

Polly giggled again. "And you're so modest, too. All great men are like that."

"What's your opinion of the Stirling engine?" Freeman asked Fonzie.

Fonzie peered at him blankly for a second, then brightened. "Oh, you mean Tootsie Sterling's Harley. It's got carbon in the valves."

"No, I'm talking about the Stirling engine. It's a concept developed by Robert Stirling in 1816."

"Freeman is interested in mechanics, too," Polly told Fonzie.

"From the theoretical standpoint," Freeman said. "That's why I've always been fascinated by the Stirling engine. Unlike the internal combustion engine, it's powered by heat from an *external* source."

"What's that mean? They have to build a fire under it to get it going?" Fonzie shook his head. "It'll never work."

"It has already been in use experimentally,"

Freeman said. "The main advantage is that it eliminates valves."

"No valves? What do they have in it instead?"

"Nothing. The need is eliminated."

"How long has this been going on?" Fonzie asked.

"Since 1816."

"And they still haven't got it going good?"

"As I say, it's in the experimental stage."

"I'll tell you what their trouble is," Fronzie said. "They ought to put some valves in it. That'll get it working." He turned to Polly again. "When you get ready to leave, I'm going your way, if you want a lift on my motorcycle," he said.

"Oh . . . well. . . . Freeman has his father's car."

"This is *my own* motorcycle," Fonzie told her.

"Don't you think that's chea— Unladylike, I mean," she said, "a girl riding on the back of a motorcycle?" She leaned slightly toward him. "You really ought to start thinking about how things look, Fonzie. I mean, you're not just a garage mechanic anymore. You have a future ahead of you. That's what going back to school means."

"What did I have in front of me before? A past?"

Polly giggled. "You're such a kidder."

"What college have you got in mind?" Freeman asked Fonzie.

"I don't know. Where do you think I could get the best training in grease jobs?"

"You know, you really ought to write things like that down," Polly told him. "I've read a lot of books about important people, and they always have quotations like that—funny little things they said when they were nobodies."

"It's too late," Fonzie said. "I've never been a nobody. I've always been me."

"You know what I mean—when you get to be rich and famous."

"You're getting a little ahead of me," Fonzie said. "When does this happen, this rich and famous?"

"I don't know exactly. I mean, I can't tell you the year and day and minute," Polly said. "But I can see it's going to happen. From the books I've read about rich and famous people who started out just like you. They were nobodies, then suddenly they saw the light, and the rest is history."

"Are you talking about Edison? Seeing the light?"

"That's one example," Polly said. "Once, he was just a tinkerer."

"Yeah, I get the picture," Fonzie said. "I tinker a lot."

"Edison was a genius," Freeman said.

"Yeah, you didn't catch him building any engines without any valves in them," Fonzie said. He got up. "Listen, I'm going to be riding past your house tonight," he said to Polly. "Maybe I'll stop in. Where do you live?"

"1203 Hamilton Street."

Fonzie nodded, "That's where I thought it was. That's the vicinity I expected to be in. So . . . maybe I'll see you." He glanced at Freeman, then, shaking his head in pity, walked back toward the other booth.

Potsie and Ralph had joined Richie.

"What is this, Noah's Ark?" Fonzie said, sitting down in the booth. "Where'd all the animals come from?"

"I'm just keeping your seat warm," Potsie told him.

Ralph started to rise to leave.

"Sit," Fonzie said.

Ralph sat.

"What's new ... uh, in the other booths?" Potsie asked Fonzie.

Fonzie ignored the question. "What do you know about Edison?" he asked Richie. "Did he ride a motorcycle?"

Richie thought for a moment. "I don't think so."

"That's what I figured," Fonzie said. "We're not anything alike." He turned to Potsie. "How're you in English?" he asked.

"So-so."

"Not good enough. Richie?"

"I do pretty well," Richie replied.

Fonzie opened another book and got out another fold of paper and gave it to Richie. "That's my English homework," he said. "How about biology?" he asked. "Ralph?"

"I almost flunked."

"Reach in that biology book there and get those papers," Fonzie said to Richie. "It's my homework."

"You're really taking school seriously," Potsie said to him.

"Yeah. If Richie holds up, I might even gradu-ate." He glanced over toward the other booth. "You say she's the queen, huh?"

"She goes with Freeman, though, Fonzie," Ralph said. "They're the perfect pair. He's smart and she's the head cheerleader."

Fonzie looked at him coldly. "Are you saying I'm not smart?"

"No. . . ."

"Who does Freeman's homework?" Fonzie said.

"He does."

"Who does my homework?"

"Richie."

"Who's smart?" Fonzie asked.

"You are," Ralph conceded.

Fonzie rode up to the Wilson house just shortly before sundown. He gunned his engine a few times to announce his arrival. Evidently the sound car-ried to the inside of the house, because he saw a fluttering movement at the front window cur-tains. Then, switching off the engine, he dismount-ed and walked toward the porch.

The house was modest. It had a small lawn, with healthy green grass and an iron deer. There were shutters at the windows and a swing and a rocking chair on the porch. He saw a shape at the screen door and recognized the contours. Polly was waiting for him. It was a good beginning to what he expected to become a pleasant relation-ship.

"I wondered what all that racket was," Polly said, as he stepped up onto the porch.

"What racket?" Fonzie asked. He hadn't heard anything.

"That motor."

"Oh. That wasn't any racket," he said. "That was me, blowing the carbon out of the valves."

Polly opened the screen door. "Well, anyway, it's nice to see you again."

"I told you I was going to be in the vicinity," Fonzie said, entering the house. He found himself in a small foyer. To his right was a living room. It was comfortably furnished, with the usual over-stuffed sofa and chairs and tables and lamps with cellophane-covered shades. "Nice place you got here," he said.

"I was just going to start practicing my twirl-ing," Polly told him.

"Oh. Okay. Spin around a couple times if you want to."

"My baton twirling," she explained.

"Oh, that."

"Why don't you go on into the living room," Polly said. "I'll get my baton."

"Right."

Fonzie watched Polly stride down a hallway, enjoying her way of moving, then, when she disap-peared through a doorway, he went into the living room and settled in an overstuffed chair. A few seconds later, an overly plump woman who remind-ed him somehow of Polly came tiptoeing into the room. She did not see Fonzie. And, caught up in watching her odd behavior, he did not speak.

The woman went to the front windows and pulled back the curtains and peeked out. She gasped.

Then, after closing the curtains, she tiptoed out. When she reached the foyer, she turned toward the front door. A moment later, Fonzie heard the screen open and close. Baffled, he got up and went to the windows and looked out. The woman was at his motorcycle. She was raising the kickstand.

"Fonzie. . . ?"

He looked back. Polly had returned with her baton.

"Some fat lady is stealing my bike," Fonzie told her.

Polly joined him at the windows. "That's Mother," she said coolly. "And she isn't stealing your motorcycle, she's just moving it."

"Where to?"

"She's putting it in front of the neighbor's house," Polly informed him. "She doesn't want a thing like a motorcycle in front of ours."

"What's the matter with it?"

"It's . . . Well, you know."

Fonzie shook his head. "I don't know."

"It looks chea— I mean, it looks rowdy. Not that it is. That's just an idea that people have. You know how people are. I realize how silly it is. After all, you can't tell a book by its cover. But Mother's such a worry wart. She's always so afraid of what people will think."

Fonzie nodded knowingly. "One of those."

"Of course, she's right—in a way," Polly said. "How can people know, seeing you riding around on that motorcycle, that you're really serious about life. They think the worst. They don't know that you've gone back to school and about your plans and how—"

The plump woman had reappeared. She was standing in the opening between the foyer and the living room, smiling sweetly.

"Mother, this is Arthur Fonzarelli," Polly said. "Arthur, Mother."

"Fonzie," Fonzie said to Mrs. Wilson, nodding.

"Polly's told me so much about you," Mrs. Wilson said. "I think your plans are just wonderful."

"My plans?" Fonzie said.

"Becoming a success," Polly explained.

"Oh, that." Fonzie shrugged. "It's nothing. It's in the blood. I'm a tinkerer."

"I was wondering: have you ever thought about changing the spelling of your name?" Mrs. Wilson asked.

"How? With a 'Ph' instead of an 'F?' "

"No, I was thinking of something like . . . oh, let's see . . . Fonzdale . . . or perhaps Fonz-Smythe —with a hyphen."

"How about Smythe-arelli?" Fonzie suggested. "That way I could still have the hyphen."

Mrs. Wilson beamed. "Well, there's plenty of time to talk about it," she said. "After all, you and Polly just met. I see you have your baton, dear," she said to her daughter. "Practice?"

"Yes, Mother."

"I think I'll stay and watch," Mrs. Wilson said, going to the sofa. "I like to try to see the baton while it's twirling around. It's a good eye exercise."

Fonzie sat down in the chair again. "I didn't

know cheerleaders did this baton stuff," he said. "I thought you just jumped up and down."

"I'm practicing for when I go to college," Polly told him. "You get a lot more attention if you can both cheer *and* twirl."

"The head cheerleader at State is coming to watch Polly at the next basketball game," Mrs. Wilson told Fonzie.

"She's going to scout me," Polly said.

"Scout a cheerleader? What else do you do besides twirl, play left tackle?"

Polly giggled. "Isn't he a howl, Mother?"

Mrs. Wilson chuckled. "My, yes, that was funny. Everybody knows there aren't any tackles on the baskeball team."

Polly took her place in the center of the room. "Here goes nothing," she announced.

The twirling began. Polly spun the baton expertly at her fingertips, meanwhile swaying rhythmically to the motion.

"See if you can see it as it goes by," Mrs. Wilson said to Fonzie. "Very good for the eyes."

He tried. But he soon found that his eyes were crossing.

The twirling continued . . . and continued . . . and continued . . .

Fonzie's eyes began to droop.

Polly paused and counted. One . . . two . . . three . . . four. . . . The twirling resumed.

"That's when she throws it up," Mrs. Wilson explained to Fonzie. "But, of course, she can't really do it in here. The ceiling is too low."

Once more, Polly paused and counted. One . . .

two ... three ... four. ... As before, the twirling resumed.

"She threw it up again," Mrs. Wilson told Fonzie.

"Yeah, a little of this goes a long way," he said. "I can see how it would make her throw up."

Polly giggled. "Fonzie, you slay me!"

Mrs. Wilson rose. "Well, I've had my exercises," she said. "I'll leave you children alone. Don't tire your fingers, darling," she said to her daughter, departing. "Save them for Mary Motherwell."

"Who's Mary Motherwell?" Fonzie asked Polly.

Pause. "One ... two ... three ... four. ... She's the head cheerleader at State." The twirling resumed.

"Five ... six ... seven ... eight. How about that!"

The twirling stopped. Polly sank down on the sofa. "Whew!" she said.

"Where's your father?" Fonzie asked.

"In the kitchen."

Fonzie thought a moment. "That figures," he said. He dropped the subject.

Polly patted the cushion beside her. "Why don't you come on over."

Nonchalantly, Fonzie rose. Casually, he strolled across the distance between the chair and the sofa, then sat down beside Polly.

She looked deep into his eyes. "I've been wanting to do this ever since this afternoon," she said. "Give me your hand."

Fonzie reached for her.

"No, I want to see *your* hand," she said.

"My hand? That's all?"

"That's what I said: your hand."

She took both of his hands in hers and held them out flat and peered at the nails. "Just what I suspected," she said. "Dirt."

Fonzie looked at his nails. "That's not dirt, that's grease," he said. "I changed a carburetor before I came over here."

Polly rose. "Don't move," she said, leaving. "I'll get some sudsy water and I'll be right back."

"What do you mean, don't move?" Fonzie called after her. "What if I get an itch?"

But she was gone.

Fonzie looked at his nails again. Okay, so they had a little grease under them. He tried to remember what Freeman Locke's nails had looked like, but couldn't. He could imagine, though. They were probably pink. That was the difference between theory and practice, between knowing how engines worked on paper and how they worked in the shop.

Polly returned, carrying a shallow bowl of soapy water. She sat down on the couch again, placed the bowl on her lap, then took Fonzie's hands and put them in the water to soak.

"How long does this take?" he asked.

"Not long."

"What comes next?"

"Well, when they're clean," she said, "I'll file them, then buff them. And I want to do something about those cuticles."

Fonzie shook his head.

"Hands are very important," Polly told him.

"Smiles and hands, that's how people judge people. All the really successful people have bright smiles and clean fingernails. Fonzie, you really ought to smile more. Smile for me."

"I can't do it with my hands in water," he told her.

"Yes, you can. Try."

"I can only smile when I've got something to smile about," Fonzie said.

"That's silly. If you're going to be really successful, you've got to smile all the time—the way I do."

"Is that what you're doing? I thought that was just how your face was built."

"Of course not," she said. "I work very hard on my smile. Just like I practice twirling. And, no matter what happens, or what anybody says to me, I keep smiling. People love me for my smile."

Fonzie studied her smile. "You've got some spinach between your teeth," he told her.

The smile vanished.

FOUR

As Richie and Potsie were approaching the school grounds, they heard the rumble of a motorcycle behind them. A moment later, Fonzie went by, with Trudy behind him on the seat of his cycle.

"I thought Fonzie was making a play for Polly Wilson," Potsie said.

"I guess he is. I keep seeing them together in the halls."

"What's he doing with Trudy?"

"Maybe he keeps her on the bench—just in case," Richie said.

"You know, I get the feeling that Fonzie doesn't like me," Potsie said.

"Nah, he likes you. He's just had a lot on his mind lately. He's only said one bad thing about you that I can remember."

"Oh, good," Potsie said, relieved. Then he scowled. "What? What did he say about me?"

"Nothing important," Richie replied.

"Come on, what was it?"

"You'd probably rather not know."

"Listen, will you tell me?" Potsie insisted. "I'd rather know. I'll go nuts trying to figure it out if I don't know."

"Well . . . he said you walk like a duck."

Potsie looked down at himself. "I do not."

"I'm only telling you what he said."

43

"Look at me," Potsie said. "Do I walk like a duck?"

"I didn't say it. Fonzie said it."

"Yeah, well . . . there's a thing or two I could tell him, too," Potsie said resentfully. He looked down at himself again. "I've always walked this way," he said.

"You walk okay."

"Why'd you tell me?" Potsie complained. "Now, I *am* walking like a duck."

"You made me tell you."

"I can't walk straight," Potsie said, near panic. "Look what's happening!"

"Forget about it," Richie advised. "Put it out of your mind and, before you know it, you'll be walking the same way you always did."

"How can I *stop* thinking about it?"

"Think about something else."

"About what?"

"Anything," Richie said. "Just to get your mind off the way you walk. Think about—" He looked at one of the books he was carrying. "—about biology."

Potsie concentrated. "I'm thinking about that frog Ralph cut up in biology last week," he said.

"That'll do it."

"Oh-oh."

"What's the matter?"

"The frog got loose," Potsie said. "There it goes—hopping, hopping, it's hopping all over the room." He suddenly groaned.

"What's the matter now?"

Potsie looked down at himself again. "It hops like a duck," he said.

By then, they had reached the school yard. Fonzie and Trudy were standing beside Fonzie's motorcycle at the curb, waiting.

"Hey, Potsie, you're walking funny," Fonzie said.

"I know—like a duck."

Fonzie shook his head. "You *used* to walk like a duck," he said. "Now, you walk like a frog." He turned to Trudy. "I got some business," he said. "Go over in the grass and find me a four-leaf clover."

She went eagerly.

"You got the English homework for me?" Fonzie said to Richie.

"Sure," Richie replied, getting papers from his notebook. "And the biology homework. Fonzie . . ."

"Yeah, good buddy?"

"Well, I've been doing your homework for over a week now . . . and to tell you the truth, I don't get much time for myself any more."

"Why didn't you say something? You don't have to do it any more."

"Thanks," Richie said, grinning.

"I'll miss your biology," Fonzie told him. "The way you draw those little germs. You're kind of the Rembrandt of the bugs."

Richie gestured modestly.

"So, no more homework," Fonzie said. "But I do need a little help of a different nature."

"Sure."

"Yeah . . . you see, I need help with this history exam tomorrow," Fonzie told him.

"You want me to tutor you?"

Fonzie looked at him sideways. "What do you mean by that?"

Richie explained quickly. "Tutoring means helping you study for the test."

"Yeah, that's what I need," Fonzie said. "Come down to the garage after school. You can tutor me while I fix Cutter Margolin's headers."

"You'll be kind of busy, won't you?" Richie said. "I've got a better idea. Why don't you come over to my house for dinner and we'll study afterwards."

"Yeah, that's okay," Fonzie replied. "I'll come right from the shop." He frowned. "How's your family on fingernails?"

"In what way?" Richie asked, puzzled.

"Are they for or against grease?" Fonzie asked.

Richie was still puzzled. "I don't think the subject's ever come up," he said.

"Okay—I'll be there for dinner."

"I see you a lot with Polly Wilson," Potsie said to Fonzie.

"You got good eyes," Fonzie told him. "Too bad about your walk."

"I never see her on your motorcycle with you, though," Potsie said.

"She's a queen," Fonzie said. "Do you see the Queen of England riding around on the back of a bike?"

Potsie shook his head.

"Let me tell you about girls," Fonzie said.

"They're different. One kind is one way, another kind is another way. So, you have to handle them different. One kind," he said, nodding in Trudy's direction, "you can tell to go look for a four-leaf clover and she hops to it, no questions asked. Another kind, you have to park your cycle in front of the neighbor's house. See what I mean?"

In unison, Potsie and Richie shook their heads.

"One kind has her eye on the future, and the other kind can't see past yesterday," Fonzie said. "So, the approach has to be different. Right?"

Richie and Potsie looked at each other.

"Let me put it another way," Fonzie said. "Say you want to get to New York. With one kind of girl, you can go east, straight ahead, and get there in no time. But, with another kind, you have to go west and go all the way around the world to get there. It takes longer, but, in the end, you're in the same place—New York."

"You're going to New York?" Potsie guessed.

Fonzie shook his head in disgust. "You not only got the walk of a frog, you got the brains of a frog," he said. He whistled to Trudy. "Time's up," he called.

"I couldn't find any," she said glumly, returning.

"That's okay—you tried, that's what counts," Fonzie told her. "Hey, listen, are you free tonight?"

She beamed. "Oh, yes!"

"Good. I want you to do my homework," Fonzie said. "How are you on drawing germs?"

The first bell rang.

Richie and Potsie walked toward the school building, leaving Fonzie and Trudy standing beside the motorcycle, completing the arrangement for her to do his homework.

"Do you get the idea that Fonzie's getting a little punchy?" Potsie said to Richie.

"Nah."

"Then what was he talking about?"

"He was just saying that New York girls are different," Richie said.

"How does he know?" Potsie said. "And what does that have to do with anything?"

Richie shrugged. "I don't know. Ask him."

Potsie shook his head. "I guess I don't want to know. I got enough to worry about with my walk." He looked down at himself again. "Maybe I have my shoes on the wrong feet."

In the dining room of the Cunningham house, Richie and Joanie were setting the table, Richie putting the plates on and Joanie distributing the silverware. Their mother arrived from the kitchen with the napkins.

"I'm hungry," Joanie complained.

"I know, dear, we all are," Marion said. "But we're waiting for Richie's guest."

"He'll be here soon," Richie said.

Howard Cunningham entered from the living room. "Marion, when are we going to eat? I've seen the Early News and the Late Early News. I'm getting a little tired of hearing Ike's latest golf score."

"Richie, are you sure your friend is coming?" Marion asked. "The mashed potatoes are getting stiff."

"He'll be here. He's working on Cutter Margolin's headers."

"Oh, well, as long as it's something important," Howard said. He started back toward the living room, then hesitated. "What are headers?" he asked his son.

"I don't know. Something on a motorcycle."

"I don't suppose you know what a Cutter Margolin is, either."

"He's a guy," Richie said.

"A hood," Joanie said. "Fonzie's a hood, too."

"He is not," Richie said. "He's just ... well, worldly."

Howard Cunningham addressed Joanie. "Why do you say Richie's friend is a hood?" he asked.

"He looks like a hood."

"Oh? What does a hood look like?"

"Like Fonzie."

"Joanie, I have the feeling you're going to be a newscaster when you grow up," Howard said. "I just heard the same kind of explanation of the Korean situation on the news."

From outside came the rumble of a motorcycle engine.

"There he is now," Richie said, leaving. "I'll go meet him and bring him in."

"Be careful," Howard warned. "If he's as hungry as I am, he may bite."

"He's a hood," Joanie said.

"Dear, I don't like to hear you talk that way," her mother said. "I'm sure he's very nice."

"He drives a motorcycle and all motorcycle drivers are hoods," Joanie said.

Her father objected. "Joanie, you can't make a broad statement like that. What's your basis for it?"

"I saw 'The Wild One,' " she told him. "Fonzie's just like Marlon Brando—a hood."

"I think you ought to withhold judgment until Marlon Brando makes another picture," Howard said. "You may find out that Fonzie is really the Pope."

They heard the front door close.

"I know a hood when I see one," Joanie insisted.

Fonzie and Richie appeared. Fonzie was wearing grease-smeared coveralls.

"Out of the mouths of babes," Howard said. He spoke quietly to his wife. "Evidently Richie didn't tell him that we don't dress for dinner."

"Shh—he's a working boy," she whispered.

Fonzie, this is my parents and this is my sister Joanie," Richie said.

Fonzie nodded. "Hi-ya."

"How nice to meet you," Marion said.

"Sorry I didn't have time to put on better threads," Fonzie said, "but I got hung up. Cutter's rod is a complicated piece of machinery."

"Oh, a header is something on a rod, eh?" Howard said.

"What else?"

"I understand you're a pretty good mechanic," Howard said.

"Yeah."

"He's the best in the country," Richie said.

"Is that right?" Howard addressed Fonzie again. "Maybe you can tell me why my car makes this funny knocking noise ... A sort of clank ... clank clank ..."

"You got a four-barrel with three-hundred horses or better?" Fonzie asked.

"I don't even know what that means."

"Fonzie works mostly on hot rods, Dad," Richie said. "He's a specialist."

"Oh. Well, I guess our car isn't in that class. It's more of a cool rod." He laughed, enjoying his joke.

Fonzie stared at him.

"Just a little automobile humor," Howard said.

Fonzie nodded. "Oh."

"Actually, my car is a De Soto sedan," Howard said.

"I don't mess with De Sotos or Edsels," Fonzie told him. "You know, you got to draw the line somewhere."

"Yes ..." Howard turned to his wife. "Marion, please, let's eat!"

"It's ready," she said. "Everybody sit down and I'll bring in the food." She headed for the kitchen. "I just hope the potatotes aren't ruined."

"Just as long as they haven't turned green," Fonzie said.

They sat down at the table, with Fonzie next to Richie. Fonzie picked up the napkin from his plate and began wiping his hands.

"Grease sticks in the wrinkles on the knuckles,"

he explained, noticing that Howard Cunningham was watching him. "It's not a big problem—unless you eat with the backs of your hands. But I don't like to see grease staring up at me when I'm cutting my meat."

"I can understand that," Howard said. "Uh ... would you like to wash up?"

"I just wiped."

"Oh. You're right—why waste the water."

Marion reappeared and began putting the food on the table.

"I said a prayer for the potatoes," she said.

"You got some kind of funny religion?" Fonzie asked.

"No, it's just a family quirk," Howard said. "Instead of saying grace in the regular way, Marion prays to the potatoes."

Fonzie considered that. "What if you don't have potatoes?"

"Rhubarb, carrots, radishes, anything will do."

Marion joined them and the passing around of the food began.

"Do you have a zip-gun in your pocket?" Joanie asked Fonzie.

"No. You need one?" He reached back. "I got a crescent wrench," he said, producing it from his rear pocket. "Will that do?"

Howard handed him the bowl of mashed potatoes.

Fonzie started to dig in with the wrench, then realized what he was doing and put the wrench away and used the spoon that was protruding from the potatoes instead.

"I saw 'The Wild One,'" Joanie said to Fonzie.

"Crummy flick."

"I should say so," Marion said.

"If I was Lee Marvin," Fonzie said, passing the potatoes to Richie, "I would have cracked Brando's skull with the trophy."

Marion winced. "Oh, my goodness!"

"Not to change the subject—" Richie said.

"Feel free," his father urged.

"I was just going to say that Fonzie's doing really great in school." He turned to his friend. "Right, Fonzie?"

Fonzie shrugged.

"What do you plan to do when you get out of school?" Marion asked him.

"I don't know. I might be a cop."

"That's very admirable," Marion said, pleased. "We need more people with that attitude."

"Yeah, it's the only job I know that pays you to ride a motorcycle," Fonzie said.

Howard nodded. "I might have known."

"There's nothing in the world like the feel of a bike under you," Fonzie said. He made a twisting motion with one hand, as if revving up a motorcycle engine. "Baroom . . . baroom . . ."

Marion winced again.

"Just a little motorcycle humor," Richie said quickly.

"This is a good dinner," Fonzie told Marion.

"Oh! Thank you."

"That praying over the potatoets really did the job," Fonzie said. "They're good and stiff—just like they make at the diner."

Marion sagged.

"I'll have to try that—a little prayer—the next time I get served soupy potatoes," Fonzie said. "The chicken is good, too. Did you kill it yourself?"

"No."

"Chicken is best," Fonzie went on, "when it's killed fresh. You wring its neck—"

Howard pushed his plate away.

"—then you duck it in scalding water—"

"Excuse me," Joanie said, rising and hurrying from the table.

"—then you pick the feathers off—"

"I better see if Joanie is all right," Marion said, departing.

"—then hang it up a while and let some of the blood run out—"

Richie pushed his plate away.

"You Cunninghams are sure light eaters," Fonzie said. He leaned back in his chair and patted his belly. "But, I guess that's the way to keep in shape."

Marion returned. "Joanie's just going to be fine—in time," she said. "She has a little touch of weak stomach."

"It's going around," Howard said.

"If you're finished, Fonzie," Richie said, "I guess we can go on up to my room and study."

"Why not?"

They got up.

"Great mashed potatoes," Fonzie said to Marion. "And the chicken—"

"Don't say it!" Howard Cunningham pleaded.

Richie hurried Fonzie out the room and toward the stairs.

"What's the rush?" Fonzie asked.

"We've got a lot of studying to do."

"Oh."

They started up the steps.

"I like your folks," Fonzie told Richie.

"They seemed to like you, too."

"Why not?" Fonzie said. "We got a lot in common."

"Yeah, you all saw 'The Wild One,' " Richie said.

"Your old man don't know much about cars, though, does he?" Fonzie said, as they reached the top of the stairs, then walked toward Richie's room. "Owning a De Soto, that's the giveaway."

"What's the matter with De Sotos?"

"Ahhh . . . how can I put it? It's hard to explain. Either you know, or you don't. I guess it's something you feel. Understand?"

"I guess so," Richie replied, opening the door to his room.

"A good mechanic is like a doctor," Fonzie said, entering. "He can look at a car and size it up. And everytime I look at a De Soto, you know what goes through my head? I think: that car better make out its will." He sat down in Richie's chair. "You can give a De Soto an aspirin and tell it to get a lot of rest. But in your heart, you know it's a gone goose."

"You really dig cars, don't you," Richie said, settling on the edge of his bed.

"Some, I do, some, I don't."

"Working on them, though, I mean."

Fonzie nodded. "You know a guy that paints a picture? Or a guy that makes a statue? When he gets it all done and it's just right, he must feel great—check?"

"Sure."

"When I get a rod running right—perfect—that's the way I feel," Fonzie said. He frowned. "Listen, that's between you and me, don't tell nobody I said that."

"Why?"

"It sounds . . . you know . . ."

"Oh. Yeah." Richie reached over and picked up his history text book from his desk. "You want to get started?"

"Yeah. But you can put that book back," Fonzie said. "We're going to do it a little different than what you got in mind."

"What do you mean? How?"

"I'll do the tutoring," Fonzie said.

"But . . . what do you know about American history?"

"Nothing. That's why we're going to do it my way," Fonzie said. "What I don't know about American history, I make up for by knowing about cheating. See? It all evens out."

For a second, Richie was too stunned to respond. Then he shook his head. "Fonzie, I can't cheat."

"Hey! Would I ask a buddy to cheat?"

"Oh," Richie said, relieved. "I thought—"

"No—I'll do the cheating," Fonzie said. "I just

need you to help me, to get me over the rough spots. Here's how we'll do it. You—"

"But—" Richie began.

"Cough," Fonzie commanded.

"What?"

"Cough. You know . . . like when you got a cold. Go on, do it—cough."

Richie hacked unenthusiastically.

Fonzie shook his head. "You sound like the engine in old man Flannagan's Ford," he said. "Try it again."

Richie coughed once more, this time with more force.

"Okay, so you'll practice," Fonzie said.

"But why?"

"It's a true or false test—right? Okay, I'm on the first question. I cough. That's the signal. Then you cough back. One cough for false and two coughs for true. Get it? It's the perfect crime."

"Fonzie, it's wrong," Richie protested.

"No it isn't. That's the way it's always done—two coughs for true, one cough for false. Take my word for it. I been at this longer than you have."

"I mean it's not right."

"What's a better way?"

"We could study," Richie told him.

Fonzie peered at him incredulously for a moment. "Richie, this is important to me, so let's be serious—okay?"

"Why *not* study?"

"Look at that book," Fonzie said. "It's all crammed full of junk. How could I learn all that in time for the test? It's not fair, Richie. They're throwing all that stuff at me and I don't know any of it."

"You'd know it if you'd been studying all along," Richie countered.

"I haven't though. And the past is water over the dam. Are you going to let me fail that test— and flunk history—and drop out of school again, on account of something I can't do anything about?"

Richie frowned. "You lost me," he said. "What can't you do anything about?"

"The studying I didn't do."

"But you *can* do something about it," Richie said. "You can study now."

"Let's try the cough again," Fonzie said. "Give me a 'true.' "

Defeated, Richie coughed twice.

"You're getting better," Fonzie told him.

"It won't work," Richie said. "Mrs. Wimper will think I have T.B."

"Yeah . . . there's that. . . ."

"So, let's study," Richie said.

"I got it," Fonzie said. "You cough for the first ten questions and whistle for the rest."

"I . . . uh . . . I don't whistle too good," Richie said.

Fonzie looked at him levelly. "Somehow, I get the feeling that your heart isn't in this," he said. "What's the matter? I'm your buddy, right?"

"Sure."

"And you're my buddy."

Richie nodded.

"Buddies help each other," Fonzie said. "Look at it this way: Say you were down in the bottom of a well and couldn't get out and I came along with a rope. Got the picture?"

"Yes, but—"

"And you yell up to me, 'Hey, Fonzie, let down the rope!' What would I do? Would I yell back down to you, 'I don't let ropes down in wells too good!?' " He shook his head. "I'd send you down the rope. I wouldn't even think about it. I'd just drop the rope down. With buddies, that's how it is."

"Fonzie, there's no connection," Richie replied. "You're asking me to help you cheat."

"Okay, let me put it another way. You kind of got me into this, Richie. You said I could make it, you said you'd help me. Old buddy, I'm not making it so good. I need your help."

Richie looked away.

"Give a whistle," Fonzie said.

Feebly, Richie whistled.

"It needs work," Fonzie said, getting up. "But we got time. You think about it. You'll be whistling like the birds." He walked toward the door. "I got to go now," he said. "I told the queen I might be around in her vicinity about this time of night."

"Maybe she could tutor you," Richie suggested.

Fonzie halted. "Richie, with girls, they don't tutor you, you tutor them. And that's exactly what I got in mind—teaching her a trick or two." He opened the door. "You better get to the studying, though," he said. "I don't want you to whistle me any wrong answers. I'm depending on you, Richie."

"Fonzie—"

"Call me 'buddy.'"

"Fonzie, buddy—"

"Remember, two for true, one for false. Keep saying that to yourself until you're sure you've got it. We don't want no mistakes." He saluted casually. "See you in class, old buddy."

The door closed behind him.

FIVE

Fonzie stopped his motorcycle at the rear of the De Soto that was parked in the glow of the street lamp in front of the Wilson house. Looking toward the front windows of the house, he gunned his engine a few times—baroom . . . baroom . . . baroom—then switched it off. As he had expected, he saw movement at the windows, the fluttering of the curtains. Mrs. Wilson, he knew, was now aware of his arrival.

When he had dismounted, Fonzie circled the De Soto, inspecting it in the way that a gourmet might examine a *boeuf bourguignon* that had been smothered in catsup, with infinite disdain. Then he swaggered toward the house, where he could see Polly's silhouette waiting at the screen door.

"Who's heap?" Fonzie asked, mounting the porch.

"The car? Oh, that's Freeman's dad's." Polly replied, opening the screen door.

"What's it out there for? To scare away stray dogs?" Fonzie asked, entering.

Polly giggled. "Oh, Fonzie, you're a scream."

Fonzie looked into the living room. Freeman Locke was sitting on the sofa.

"Go on in," Polly said. "You can help. I'm practicing the new cheer, and Freeman is answering."

"Yeah? What's the question?"

"Oh, you know what I mean." Polly took his hand, towing him into the living room. "Look who's here!" she said to Freeman Locke.

"Hi, fella," Freeman said grudgingly.

"The same to you," Fonzie responded.

"Sit here beside Freeman," Polly said to Fonzie. "I'll give the cheer and you two can—"

Fonzie, having heard a faint sound from the direction of the foyer, had turned away. He saw Mrs. Wilson tiptoeing toward the front door.

"Fonzie, pay attention," Polly said.

"Yeah, just a minute."

Fonzie went to the front windows. He pulled back the curtain. In the light from the street lamp, he saw Mrs. Wilson going toward his motorcycle. Obviously, she intended to move it again, to park it in front of the neighbor's house. Fonzie closed the curtain.

"A De Soto she lets sit," Fonzie said, shaking his head in dismay, "but a bike—precision tuned—she moves. I don't get it."

"I told you how she is," Polly said. "Come on, let's practice the cheer."

"What's the matter with a De Soto?" Freeman said to Fonzie.

"What's the matter with a two-dollar watch?" Fonzie replied. "It's junk."

"Come on, now, fella," Freeman said. "That De Soto has aerodynamic design. The wind resistance is practically zero."

"The wind resistance on anything that don't move is practically zero," Fonzie said.

"Boys!" Polly said. "Are we going to practice or aren't we?"

Fonzie sat down on the sofa—as far away from Freeman as possible.

"Closer. Get together. Be a crowd," Polly said.

"Two can't be a crowd," Fonzie said. He glared at Freeman. "It's three that's a crowd," he said.

"There were only two here until you came," Freeman replied.

"Boyeeeees!" Polly pleaded.

There was the sound of the screen door closing. Then Mrs. Wilson appeared in the foyer. She stopped in the opening to the living room.

"Such a lovely evening," she said, beaming. "I just had to take a little stroll."

"Yeah, you touch my bike again, and I'm going to break both your arms," Fonzie said.

Mrs. Wilson stared at him, stunned.

Polly giggled. "Mother, you know what a comedian Fonzie is," she said.

The look of shock passed from Mrs. Wilson's face. "A sense of humor is such an asset," she said. "A laugh a day keeps the gloomies away." She chuckled. "Oh, my!"

"Mother, I'm still practicing the new cheer," Polly said. "Why don't you sit on the sofa with Fonzie and Freeman and help be the crowd?"

"She's a crowd herself," Fonzie said.

Mrs. Wilson laughed. "Oh, Fonzie, you're a laugh a minute," she said, seating herself between him and Freeman Locke.

"I composed this cheer myself," Polly told Fonzie. "Here's how it goes: First, we do the letters,

spelling out Jefferson—with a cheer after each letter. Like, you know: J-Rah! E-Rah! F-Rah! and
on. Then we come in with the verse, which goes
like this: Hit that basket/Make a score!/
Cheer for the ref/Cheer for Jeff. Then we end it
with: Jefferson! Jefferson! Rah! Rah! Rah!" She
took a breath. "Okay?"

" 'Cheer for the ref?' " Fonzie asked.

"It won't hurt to butter up the referee a little,
will it?" she said. "I'll go through it once for
you," she said, "so you can get the idea."

Polly took her stance, feet apart, then began
the chant, punching the air on each Rah!

"J-Rah! E-Rah! F-Rah! F-Rah! E-Rah! R-Rah
S-Rah! O-Rah! N-Rah!
Jefferson High!
Hit that basket . . . make a score!
Cheer for the ref!
Cheer for Jeff!
Jefferson! Jefferson! Rah! Rah! Rah!"

"You want *me* to say that?" Fonzie asked.

"Along with me and Mom and Freeman," she
replied.

"There's always some guy in the crowd who
don't yell," Fonzie said. "I'll be him."

"Fonzeeeee, pleeeeeeze . . ."

He sighed. "Okay, okay."

Polly began the cheer again. Fonzie, Mrs. Wilson and Freeman Locke chanted along with her.
But in the middle she suddenly stopped.

"Who said 'Hit the ref?' " she asked.

"Ain't that the way it goes?" Fonzie replied innocently.

"It's 'Hit that basket.' "

"Oh."

Polly began again. This time she was in the middle of the spelling out of the school name when she stopped.

"Fonzie, you said 'Z-Rah!' There's no 'z' in Jefferson."

"I'm a lousy speller."

"Maybe it would be better if I practiced with the other cheerleaders," Polly decided.

"Yes, I think that's best," Mrs. Wilson said, rising. "It takes professionals to really do a cheer right. Would you children like some refreshments?" she asked. "I'll bring in some milk and cookies."

"You know, that's just what I had on my mind," Fonzie said. "I always like to wind up a cheer with a cookie and shot of milk."

Mrs. Wilson chuckled. "Fonzie, you're a riot!"

When she had gone, Polly took her place on the sofa between Fonzie and Freeman.

"Well . . . here we are . . ." Polly said.

"Yeah, the whole crowd, all three of us," Fonzie said. He looked past her at Freeman. "How's that guy and his nutty engine?" he said. "Did you tell him to put some valves in it if he wants to get it working?"

"He's dead," Freeman replied.

"That's one way to stay out of the booby hatch."

"That's what they said about Fulton," Freeman countered.

"Yeah? What'd he do. Come up with an engine without a starter?"

Polly giggled. "Oh, Fonzie, you know what Fulton invented."

He looked at her blankly. "The baton?"

"No, silly! Don't you remember? The cotton gin."

"How would I know that?" Fonzie said. "I never drink anything stronger than beer."

"The steam engine," Freeman said.

"Speaking of that," Polly said, "I got a letter from Mary Motherwell today. It's definite now, she's coming to the game to scout me for State."

"No kidding?" Fonzie said. "Speaking of that, I put new headers on Cutter Margolin's rod today. Wait'll you hear it. It purrs like a rhinoceros."

"I see you have grease under your fingernails again," Polly said.

"What did you mean when you said that about a De Soto?" Freeman asked Fonzie. "My dad's getting a new one."

"There's one born every minute," Fonzie said.

"Mary Motherwell started cheering when she was three years old," Polly said.

"What's a kid three years old got to cheer about?"

"She's been cheering the State teams since she was a freshman," Polly said. "She's 36-4-2."

"Man, that's a skinny waist," Fonzie said.

"That's not her measurements," Polly said. "It's the teams' records."

"Aerodynamically speaking, the De Soto is ahead of its time," Freeman said.

"It has its moments when it's okay," Fonzie said.

"Ha! You admit it!"

"Yeah, it's not bad when it's rolling downhill with the motor turned off."

"Mary Motherwell has a throat specialist standing by at every game—just like a team physician," Polly said.

"That figures," Fonzie said. "All that yelling, her throat has to get Rah!"

Mrs. Wilson reappeared with a tray of refreshments.

"Milk and cookies!" she announced exuberantly, placing the tray on the table at the end of the sofa. "I hope you boys like raisin cookies."

"As long as the raisins don't crawl," Fonzie said.

Mrs. Wilson chuckled. "You're such a card, dear!" She took a book from the tray. "I have a little present for you," she told Fonzie. "I got it at the lending library today. You can keep it for a whole week."

Fonzie accepted the book from her. " 'Let A Smile Be Your Ticket?' " he said, reading the title. "Where am I going?"

"It's a book on self-improvement. How to get to the top," she told him. "Keep smiling—that's the message. But it also has a lot of other little hints. On grooming, for instance. It pays to look well."

"I didn't know I looked sick."

She laughed. "Oh, my, that's funny."

"I read the first chapter," Polly told Fonzie. "It has a wonderful example in it. It's about a man whose house and car and factory were all destroyed on the same day in a hurricane. But he just kept smiling. And today he's rich."

"How'd he work that?"

"He was heavily insured," Polly explained.

"Speaking of that," Mrs. Wilson said, "I was thinking to myself the other day: companies ought to have cheerleaders. Imagine how down in the dumps that insurance company felt when it had to pay that man all that money. If it had a cheerleader, it would have somebody to pep everybody up again."

"Good cookies," Freeman said.

"Watch the milk, though—it's got a kick," Fonzie said.

Polly giggled. "Fonzie, you're the life of the party!"

"I wonder if Mary Motherwell has ever thought about offering herself to a company," Mrs. Wilson said.

"De Soto could use her," Fonzie said. "That must be a sad bunch."

"Actually, I don't think Mary ought to go into business," Polly said. "She ought to be our inspiration. I see her, for instance, as cheerleader for the United Nations."

"Yeah, they need somebody even more than De Soto," Fonzie said.

"She could open the way," Polly said. "Then we who follow could go into business."

"What business are you going into, Fonzie?" Mrs. Wilson asked.

"Well, I was thinking about being a cop," he said. "But now that you gave me this book, that's changed. I don't think you can be a cop and smile, too."

Mrs. Wilson turned to her daughter. "Is he joking again?" she asked.

"Of course, Mother. Why would a person with Fonzie's drive want to be a policeman?"

"So I could drive a motorcycle," Fonzie said.

"See?" Polly said to her mother. "He was joking. I told you, he's the self-made man kind. When he sees something he wants, he goes after it. The way he came back to school. He saw that the path to success leads through the forest of higher education, and now he's going after it." She smiled at Fonzie. "Isn't that right?"

"If you want to know the truth," Fonzie said, "I was thinking more about the girls."

Polly giggled.

Mrs. Wilson chuckled. "Precious," she said. She turned to her daughter once more. "Don't forget about your beauty sleep, darling."

"The boys were just going," Polly told her.

Freeman rose.

But Fonzie remained seated. "I got all night," he said. He indicated Freeman. "Let the kid go on," he said. "I'll hang around a while."

Freeman sat down.

"Fonzie, if I don't get a full ten hours sleep, I lose finger dexterity," Polly said. "I might drop my baton while I'm trying out for Mary Mother-well. It's my big chance."

Fonzie shrugged. "Okay." He addressed Freeman. "You first," he said.

"I got up first last time, this time it's your turn," Freeman responded.

"We'll do it together," Fonzie said. "Ready? On the count of three."

"Ready."

"One . . . two . . . *three*!"

Fonzie started to rise.

Freeman rose to his feet once more.

But Fonzie had been faking. He was still seated.

"That's cheating!" Freeman protested.

"I'm a self-made man," Fonzie said. "That's the way I made me."

"Fonzeeeee, pleeeeeeeze. . . ," Polly begged.

He got up. "We go out the door together, the same way, okay?" he said to Freeman.

"No cheating."

"Would I pull a trick like that again? Twice?"

"Just don't try it," Freeman warned.

"What would you do to me?" Fonzie asked. "Make me ride in your De Soto?" He led the way to the foyer. "Thanks for the cookies and milk," he said to Mrs. Wilson. "It made my night."

"I'm glad you liked them."

"I didn't say that."

Polly giggled.

Her mother chuckled.

They reached the screen door.

"Ready?" Fonzie said to Freeman.

"Ready!"

Fonzie pushed the door open. "After you," he said.

Freeman went striding past him, out onto the porch, where, abruptly, he halted, realizing what he had done.

"You cheated again!" Freeman said.

"You got to learn to smile about things like that," Fonzie replied, following him out.

"Oh! Your book! You forgot it!" Mrs. Wilson said to Fonzie.

"You're right—I did," Fonzie said, going on. He took Freeman's arm and they went down the steps together.

SIX

The living room of the Cunningham house was dark except for the faint glow from the television set. Seated in front of the screen were Howard and Marion. Howard's eyes were about to close. Marion's were wide open. On the screen, a wrestler named Prince Edward Island had another wrestler named Immaculate Ferdinand in a toe hold. The Prince was wearing what he had described to the audience before the match began as gold lamb trunks trimmed in blue sequins and high-heeled ankle-height satin boots. Immaculate Ferdinand had on silk trunks, a silk cape and a phosphorus-coated wire halo.

"I can't believe it isn't real," Marion said. "They seem to be suffering so."

"Marion they take acting lessons from Bette Davis to learn that."

"I think Prince Edward is getting loose!" Marion said.

"We're the ones who are loose, sitting here watching this," Howard said. "We're loose in the head."

On the screen, Prince Edward Island, free, lumbered to his feet. Immaculate Ferdinand had retreated to a neutral corner.

"Isn't it about time one of them threw the other one out of the ring?" Howard said.

"Oh, is it that late?"

The Prince and Immaculate were now circling each other in the center of the ring.

"Yeah, I recognize the dance," Howard said. "Which one will go out, do you think?"

"Immaculate was booed the most," Marion said.

"It'll be him, then."

Immaculate lunged at the Prince and they began grappling awkwardly. The crowd cheered and booed.

"I hope it isn't Immaculate," Howard said. "He could hurt himself if he lands on that halo."

Prince Edward Island was trying to pick Immaculate up to twirl him over his head. But he was having trouble. Immaculate finally gave him an assist, climbing up onto his shoulders.

The crowd booed and cheered.

"Around and around he goes," Howard said sleepily, as the Prince began spinning Immaculate over his head.

"I wish you hadn't said that about that halo," Marion said, fretting. "Now, I'm worried."

"It may not be a halo," Howard said. "Maybe it's a spring and he'll bounce back."

Prince Edward Island released his adversary. Immaculate Ferdinand went flying from the ring and landed in the audience.

"Now, it gets good," Howard said, leaning forward.

The ringsiders were attacking Immaculate, the men beating him with their fists, the women pummeling him with the umbrellas they had brought to the match for that purpose. Ferdinand flailed back at them, meanwhile struggling to get back into the ring.

"I like the lady with the fur neckpiece," Howard said. "She's got a great left umbrella."

"Oh! It's sickening!" Marion said.

"Yeah, great, isn't it!"

Immaculate Ferdinand got hold of the ropes and started to pull himself up. But Prince Edward Island, recognizing the cue, bit him on the knuckles, forcing him to let go, then shoved him back into the crowd. Again, the ringsiders attacked.

"That's just too savage," Marion said, rising. She went to the set and turned it off.

"What happened!" Howard said, as the light from the screen faded. "It's night!"

Marion turned on a table lamp. "Yes, and time to—" she began. She had discovered that Richie was in the room. He was standing by the doorway, leaning against the wall. "Oh, dear!" she said. "You gave me a fright, Richie. I didn't know you were here."

"I just came down," he said.

"Is something the matter?"

"No," he said listlessly.

"Are you sure?"

"I'm sure, Mom."

"You really ought to be in bed, Richie. Tomorrow's a school day."

"I couldn't sleep."

"Well . . .." Marion looked at Howard. "I think I'll go on up," she said. "You boys better get to bed, too."

"Thank you, Marion," Howard said.

"What did I do?"

"You called me a boy," he replied. "I haven't been called a boy since that day last year when I was carrying our bags through the train station and that guy mistook me for a porter."

"Oh, yes, that terrible man."

"I think he's now Immaculate Ferdinand," Howard said. "I knew there was something familiar about him. Maybe it was the halo. The guy at the station's didn't look very permanent either."

"Well . . . goodnight . . ."

"Goodnight."

" 'Night, Mom," Richie said.

"Did you see the wrestling match?" Howard asked Richie, when Marion had gone.

"Part of it . . . sort of . . ."

"Something on your mind?"

"No."

Howard indicated the chair that Marion had vacated. "Want to sit down and not talk about it?" he said.

"I was just thinking," Richie said, moving toward the chair. "How did you like Fonzie?"

"Well, I hate to admit it after what he said about my De Soto, but . . . well, he's sort of likable . . . for a hood."

"He's not a hood," Richie said, sitting down on the arm of the chair.

"I know he's not, Richie. That was a feeble attempt at humor."

"He's really a great guy," Richie said.

"I'll take your word for it."

"He acts kind of tough, but there isn't anything he wouldn't do for you," Richie said. "I really think of him as a friend."

"Good."

"If I asked him to do something for me, he'd do it," Richie said. "I mean, he wouldn't ask questions. He'd just do it. That's the kind of a guy he is."

Howard nodded. "The salt of the earth."

"Right."

Silence.

"He's really a great mechanic, too," Richie said. "Take any kind of a car to him, or a motorcycle, and he can fix it."

"Even if there's nothing wrong with it, I'll bet," Howard said.

"And you can talk to him," Richie went on. "If you've got something on your mind, you know, that you wouldn't talk to another guy about, you can talk to Fonzie about it. He listens. And if it's not funny, he doesn't joke. You really can *talk* to him."

"I think I've got it," Howard said. "He's the salt of the earth, he's the world's best mechanic, and he listens. Anything else?"

Richie thought for a moment. "He can spit through his teeth."

"Richie, why are you trying so hard to sell me on Fonzie?" Howard asked. "I told you: I like him."

"No reason in particular," Richie said. "But if you've got a friend like Fonzie—a guy who'll do anything for you, no questions asked—you ought to be willing to do the same for him—right?"

"That depends," Howard said.

"What do you mean?"

"Well, I'm not sure that in all cases a friend who will do anything you want him to for you—no questions asked—is really your friend. Suppose the something was something that was wrong for you? Wouldn't he be a better friend if he *didn't* do it?"

"How do you mean like?"

"Well, say you were my friend and I came to you and told you I needed money desperately and asked you to help me rob a bank. What kind of a favor would you be doing me if you *did* help me do that?"

"Fonzie didn't ask me to help him rob a bank."

"I didn't say he did, Richie. I was giving you an example."

"Yeah, but robbing a bank is pretty serious."

"You're right," Howard said. "I've changed my mind, I won't ask you to do it."

Silence again.

"Do you still remember when you were in school?" Richie asked.

"How could I forget? George Washington had the seat right across from me."

"What did you think about grades?" Richie asked.

"In what way?"

"How important grades are, I mean."

"It depended," Howard replied. "If I got a bad grade, I thought grades were stupid. If I got a good grade, I thought grades meant everything."

"But suppose a guy got a good grade but he didn't get it honestly. The whole world wouldn't come to an end, would it?"

"Are you cheating in school, Richie?"

Richie shook his head.

"Good."

"You didn't answer the question."

"I didn't care much for it," Howard said. "It was loaded. No, of course the world wouldn't come to an end if you got a good grade but didn't get it honestly. That isn't to say that it's all right to cheat, though." He looked at his son narrowly. "You're sure you're not cheating in school?"

"No. Honest."

"All right."

"Those guys on TV are cheating," Richie said.

"Who?"

"The wrestlers. They're not really wrestling."

"I know that, Richie. Everybody knows that. It's a show."

"If everybody knows it, how come those people at the wrestling match get so worked up about it?" Richie asked.

"Well . . . maybe not everybody knows . . ." He looked away. "Anybody with any brains knows it, though."

"It's okay to cheat people, then, if they don't have any brains?"

"Uh . . . Richie, how did we get on this subject? I thought we were talking about cheating in school."

"It's sort of the same thing," Richie said. "If

it's okay to cheat on TV and fool people and get away with it, why isn't it okay to do it in school?"

Howard sighed. "You know you're ruining the wrestling matches for me? And that isn't easy, I didn't like them in the first place."

Richie got up. "I guess I'll go to bed."

"Richie . . ."

He halted. "Yeah?"

"The answer to your question is: it isn't right to cheat on TV *or* in school. But whether you do it or not is something you have to decide for yourself. The fact that they cheat on TV doesn't make it right for somebody else to cheat in school."

"People do it, though."

"People swallow goldfish, too, Richie."

"Yeah, well . . ." He moved on.

"I really did like Fonzie," Howard said.

"He's a good guy."

"If he's easy to talk to," Howard said, "maybe you ought to talk to him about cheating. He'll probably tell you the same thing I just told you."

Richie halted again and looked back. "Why do you say that?"

"Well, it figures. The salt of the earth, a great mechanic, a sympathetic ear—he sounds like a guy who has his head on straight."

"You think he'd be against cheating, huh?"

"I would almost guarantee it," Howard said. "And, Richie, I'm a pretty good judge of people."

Richie smiled. "Goodnight, Dad."

"Goodnight, son."

SEVEN

"You're not listening," Potsie complained, as he and Richie approached the school yard.

"What?"

"I said you're not listening. I'm talking and you're not hearing a thing I say."

"I heard you," Richie replied. "I said 'What?' didn't I?"

"Okay, what have I been talking about?"

"Uhhhhh . . ."

"I was talking about you," Potsie told him. "You've been going around in a fog. You don't hear anything anybody says."

"I got a lot of things on my mind," Richie said.

"What?"

"Things." Richie halted and scanned the school yard, where students were gathered in small groups, waiting for the first bell to ring. "Do you see Fonzie?"

"I see his motorcycle," Potsie said.

"I can't talk to his motorcycle."

"Why not?—I can talk to a blank wall," Potsie said.

"What?"

"That's what talking to you is like lately—like talking to a blank wall," Potsie said.

"There he is!" Richie said, pointing.

Fonzie was sitting under a large tree, leaning

against the trunk. *Hot Rod* magazine was open in front of his face.

"Yeah, that's him," Potsie said. "I recognize the literature."

Richie and Potsie walked toward the tree.

"Nobody's with him," Potsie said. "That's funny. Usually some girl is hanging around. Where's Trudy?"

"How do I know?"

"It's funny, that's all," Potsie said.

As they got closer to the tree, Fonzie glanced up. He quickly closed the magazine and put it behind him.

"Oh-oh!" Potsie said. "Did you see that? You know what that means don't you? He's hiding something behind *Hot Rod* magazine. What do you think? One of those books?"

"What kind of books?"

"You know."

Richie shook his head. "Nah . . ."

"I'll bet," Potsie said. "I used to hide Superman Comics behind my history book. But I'll tell you one thing, that wasn't a history book Fronzie was hiding behind *Hot Rod*."

"Maybe it's Superman Comics," Richie said.

"Cut it out. It's one of those you-know books. Boy, I'd like to see that."

They reached Fonzie.

"Hi," Richie said.

Fonzie nodded.

"How come nobody's around?" Potsie asked.

"You ever heard of privacy?" Fonzie asked.

"Fonzie, I've got to talk to you about something," Richie said.

"Richie, this is my privacy hour."

"Yeah, but—"

"No 'buts' Richie."

"How about a look at your *Hot Rod* magazine?" Potsie said, grinning.

"You're too young," Fonzie told him.

Potsie nudged Richie. "What'd I tell you?"

"What *did* you tell him?" Fonzie asked.

"Oh. Nothing, Fonzie. Nothing important. I was just saying that it's a nice day to sit under a tree."

"How about after school?" Richie said to Fonzie. "Could I talk to you then? It's important. It's about you-know-what."

Fonzie looked perplexed.

"About coughing and whistling," Richie said.

"You lost your whistle again?"

"No."

"Then everything's set," Fonzie said. "There's nothing to talk about."

The bell rang.

"We better get going," Potsie said.

"Yeah, go," Fonzie told them.

"After school?" Richie said to Fonzie.

"I got something to do after school," Fonzie replied. "I got to take the queen to the railroad station."

"Is she leaving town?" Potsie asked.

"If you *got* to know, Mary Motherwell is coming in on the train," Fonzie said.

"Who's—"

Fonzie interrupted. "You're making a real mess out of my privacy hour," he told Potsie.

Potsie backed away. "Sorry . . ."

"Fonzie, I've *got* to talk to you," Richie said.

"The first spare minute I get, it's yours," Fonzie said.

"Well . . . all right . . ."

"You better get to class," Fonzie said. "You don't want to miss anything—not with that test coming up. Right?"

"Yeah, right," Richie said glumly. "What about you? You're supposed to be in class, too."

"I'm not done with my privacy hour," Fonzie said.

Potsie pulled at Richie's sleeve. "Come on."

Reluctantly, Richie gave in. He and Potsie turned away and walked toward the entrance to the school. The school yard was now nearly deserted.

Potsie looked back. "He's at it again," he reported to Richie. "Boy, would I like to see what he's got behind that magazine!"

They reached the door and entered and set out along the corridor toward the history classroom.

"What was that about coughing and whistling?" Potsie asked Richie.

"Nothing."

"Don't kid me. Somebody has T.B.," Potsie said. "Who is it?"

"Nobody. Forget it."

They reached the classroom just as the second bell rang. Mrs. Wimper was writing on the board, posting the night's homework assignment. Richie and Potsie went quickly to their seats.

"Good morning," Mrs. Wimper said, turning from the board. "Let's begin the day with a review of Chapter Seventeen. Why did President Truman say that the conflict in Korea was not a war but a police action?"

Freeman Locke spoke up. "Because he said the North Koreans were bandits," he said.

"I thought it was because he blew the whistle on them," Potsie said.

Mrs. Wimper peered at him. "Pardon?"

"The police whistle," Potsie said.

Mrs. Wimper shook her head. "Actually, neither of you have the real reason," she said. "He called it a police action because that allowed him to—"

The door opened. Fonzie entered. He strolled toward his seat.

"Fonzie . . . do you have a 'late' slip?" Mrs. Wimper asked.

"What's that?" he answered, easing into his seat.

"It's a slip. You get it in the office. It's your permission to come to class late."

"I'm already here," Fonzie said.

"Well, yes, that's true, but—"

"What do I want to go to the office and get a piece of paper and come back for?" Fonzie said. "That's dumb. I'll miss class. What'm I in school for? To run back and forth from here to the office or to find out what's going on in class?"

"I suppose you have a point. However—"

"You got some old 'late' slips laying around?" Fonzie said. "Just put my name on one of them."

"Well, I imagine we could make an exception this—" She closed her eyes for a moment and shook her head. "Where was I?" she said, facing the class again.

"Harry was whistling up the cops," Potsie said.

"Oh, yes. Now, as I was saying, his real reason . . ."

As Mrs. Wimper resumed the explanation, Polly Wilson, who was seated behind Fonzie, leaned forward and whispered to him.

"Did you get the car?" she asked.

"It's all set," Fonzie replied.

"Is it nice?"

"The classiest job in town," he told her.

"I hope so. It's really important to impress Mary Motherwell," Polly whispered.

"What's she going to pick you for, how good you can yell or how classy your car is?"

"Fonzie, you don't understand. Appearances count."

Mrs. Wimper interrupted. "Fonzie! Polly! Is that a private discussion or can anyone get in on it?"

"Nah, it's not private," Fonzie replied. "We're talking about going to the station to pick up Mary Motherwell when she comes in on the train."

"I didn't mean—" Mrs. Wimper began.

"She's coming from State to hear Polly yell," Fonzie went on. "Polly made up a new cheer for it." He turned in his seat. "Tell her how it goes," he said to Polly.

"Well—"

"This is a history class!" Mrs. Wimper protested.

"It's a short cheer," Polly said, rising. She addressed the class. "First, we do the letters, spelling out Jefferson, with a cheer after each letter," she said. "Like, you know, J-Rah! E-Rah! F-Rah! . . ."

Mrs. Wimper sat down at her desk. Covering her face with her hands, she shook her head in utter despair.

Fonzie parked Cutter Margolin's hot rod in front of the Wilson house, then got out and went to the door and knocked. There was no answer. He looked through the screen and saw a shadowy movement at the rear of the house. Again, he knocked. As before, there was no response. So he opened the screen door and stepped into the foyer.

"Hey!" he called.

Mrs. Wilson appeared at the far end of the hall. "There you are!" she said, approaching.

"I knocked, but I couldn't raise anybody," Fonzie said.

"I didn't hear you, dear. Polly is upstairs." Mrs. Wilson halted and looked at Fonzie in dismay. "You're not dressed," she said.

Fonzie looked down at his grease-smeared coveralls. "What do you think this is, my nude suit?"

"But you're so messy!"

"I gave the car a final tune-up before I brought

it over," he explained. "I know how important this is to Polly, so I thought I wouldn't take no chances."

"Oh, yes, the car—it *is* important," Mrs. Wilson said. "I hope it's nice," she said, looking past Fonzie, through the screen door. "Appearances are so—" She screamed. "What's that!"

Fonzie turned and looked out the front door. "What? I don't see nothing."

"That wreck!" Mrs. Wilson shrieked.

Fonzie faced her again, looking hurt. "That's Cutter Margolin's rod," he told her. "It's the classiest heap in town."

Mrs. Wilson screamed again. "Polleeeeeee!"

Polly came racing down the stairs. "What happened!"

Mrs. Wilson pointed through the doorway. "Look! That's the car!"

Polly turned toward the door. She screamed.

"How come all of a sudden everybody's forgetting to smile?" Fonzie asked.

"I'm ruined!" Polly howled. "How can I meet Mary Motherwell in . . . in . . . in *that!*"

"It's the classiest heap in town," Fonzie said. "Four barrels, brand-new headers—"

"It doesn't even have a top!"

"Yeah, it's cut down," Fonzie said.

"It's a monster!" Mrs. Wilson wailed.

Fonzie nodded, smiling proudly. "Yeah, I told you it's the classiest heap in town."

Polly went out onto the porch. "Isn't there something you can do to it?" she said to Fonzie.

"What can you do to something that's perfect?"

"It's horrible!" Polly told him. "I can't—"

A new De Soto had pulled up behind the hot rod.

"Saved!" Polly Shrieked, leaving the porch and running toward the De Soto.

Freeman Locke got out. "How do you like it?" he said. "Dad just got it today."

"Freeman, you've got to take me to the station to meet Mary Motherwell," Polly said. "It's a matter of life and death."

"Sure."

Fonzie and Mrs. Wilson joined them.

"What a lovely shine!" Mrs. Wilson said, admiring the exterior.

"How far did you drive it so far?" Fonzie asked Freeman. "A couple miles? I bet the carburetor is full of carbon already."

"Freeman, please, let's go," Polly said. "If I'm not there to meet Mary Motherwell, she might turn around and go back."

"Don't worry, I'll get you there," Freeman said, opening the door on the passenger's side. "When we get to Main Street, I'll open 'er up. You'll really see some speed."

"Be careful!" Mrs. Wilson cautioned.

"Don't worry," Fonzie told her. "When he talks about speed and a De Soto, he's talking about, tops, thirty-five miles-per."

"You coming, fella?" Freeman called to Fonzie, getting in behind the wheel.

"Fonzie still has on his work clothes," Polly told Freeman. "Come on, let's go."

Freeman hesitated a second. He looked at Fonzie, then at Polly, then started the engine. The De Soto pulled out and moved on up the street. A few moments later, it turned a corner, heading for Main Street.

"I know how disappointed you are," Mrs. Wilson said to Fonzie.

"Yeah, I sure wanted to meet that Mary Motherwell," he said. "How often do you see somebody with a four-inch waist."

"But remember," Mrs. Wilson said, "every little setback is a lesson in life."

"No kidding."

"Oh, yes. We can learn from our mistakes. For instance, you learned something today, I'm sure."

"Yeah, you're right," Fonzie said sadly. "They're still finding suckers around to buy those De Sotos."

"That's not what I mean, Fonzie. What I mean is: there's a right way to do things and a wrong way. You did the wrong thing, and Polly had to leave you behind. Freeman did the right thing, and now he's her knight in shining armor."

"That armor's got a lousy carburetor," Fonzie said.

"Oh, my. I'm afraid life's little lesson has passed you by."

"No, I learned something," Fonzie said.

"Good. What have you learned?"

"I should have gone over to Freeman Locke's house and let the air out of his tires before I showed up here," Fonzie said, getting into Cutter Margolin's rod. "I didn't think ahead."

"Fonzie—"

A blast came from the hot rod.

Mrs. Wilson screamed again and ran for the house.

Fonzie drove to the corner, then turned in the direction of Main Street. When he had gone a few blocks, he saw a De Soto parked at the curb ahead. It was Freeman Locke's. Fonzie stopped behind it. The hood of the De Soto was up and Freeman was looking baffledly at the engine. Polly was standing beside him, fretting.

"Fonzie! Do something!" Polly begged.

"You want me to drive you to the station?"

"No! Fix Freeman's car!"

"I don't work on De Sotos," he told her. "That's where I draw the line."

"Then tell me what to do and *I'll* do it," Freeman said.

"You want me to tell you what to do?"

"Yes."

"Trade this De Soto in on a bicycle," Fonzie said.

"Fonzeeeee, pleeeeeeze . . ." Polly pleaded. "If you don't, I'll be late! I'll miss Mary Motherwell! I may never have a chance like this again."

"Tell you what you do," Fonzie said. "Just leave the engine here and drive the shine to the station."

"Fonzie, don't be nasty," Polly said, pouting.

"You're not smiling again," Fonzie told her.

She suddenly brightened. "If you fix Freeman's

car, you can come to the station with us to pick up Mary Motherwell," she said, "even the way you're dressed!"

"What'll she think!" Fonzie said, in mock horror.

"Don't worry about that," Polly said. "I'll tell her that the car broke down and that you're a mechanic and we brought you along in case we had car trouble again."

"I got a better idea," Fonzie said. "Tell her you ran over me on the way to the station and you're giving me this big treat of letting me meet her so I won't sue you for leaving the accident."

Polly peered at him puzzledly.

"You brought the accident—me—along with you, Fonzie explained. "I look like I been in an accident, don't I?"

She looked at him even more closely. "Are you joking again, Fonzie?"

"It's no joke," he told her. Then he turned to the car and looked under the hood. He pointed. "See that loose cable," he said to Freeman.

Freeman nodded. "I saw it when I opened the hood. But I don't know where it goes."

Fonzie bent over to connect the cable.

"What is it?" Freeman asked.

"It's your horn cable," Fonzie told him. "De Sotos run on the horn. Disconnect the horn and a De Soto stops dead."

Polly giggled.

"It's fixed," Fonzie said, straightening. He closed the hood. "Give it a try."

Freeman and Polly got into the car. A moment later, the engine started.

"Fonzie, you're wonderful!" Polly said. Her expression became wistful. "You don't really want to come to the station with us, though, do you . . . dressed like that?"

"Hey!" Freeman said to her.

"I'm just thinking of Fonzie," she said. "He'd be embarrassed."

"She's right," Fonzie told Freeman. "If I was seen driving around in a De Soto, I'd lose every friend I got." He motioned. "Go on!"

Once more, Freeman hesitated. Then he shrugged and shifted into gear and the De Soto pulled away.

Polly put her head out the window. "Don't forget to be at the game tonight!" she called back to Fonzie. "I need every voice I can get for the cheering!"

"Yeah . . . if I'm in the vicinity. . . ," Fonzie replied.

The game had already started when Fonzie parked his motorcycle near the entrance to the school gymnasium that night. After dismounting, he stood for a moment and listened to the sounds coming from inside.

"E-Rah!"

"R-Rah!"

"S-Rah!"

"O-Rah!"

"N-Rah!"

"JEFFERSON!"

Fonzie walked toward the entrance. At first, he thought he would be the last one to arrive. Then he saw someone else approaching the doors. It was Freeman Locke.

Seeing Fonzie, Freeman halted. "I didn't think you'd be here," he said.

"Why not?"

"After the way Polly treated you today."

"Stuff like that rolls off me like water off an oil can," Fonzie said. He indicated the doors. "After you."

Freeman shook his head. "Oh, no. You pulled that on me before. After you."

Fonzie shook his head. "Either you go first, or we stand here all night."

"Suits me," Freeman said stubbornly. Then he added: "What was that cable on the car to?"

"What do you care? Believe me, it's got nothing to do with the aerodynamics."

"Maybe I want to know. Maybe I want to fix it myself if it happens again."

"It won't," Fonzie said. "The same thing never goes wrong on a De Soto twice. It's always something different. That's the way a De Soto goes— it's one part after another." He cocked an ear. "Hear that?" he said. "That creaking? That's your De Soto falling apart while it's sitting in the parking lot."

"I didn't bring it," Freeman told him. "I walked."

"I can hear it all the way from your house," Fonzie said.

"It's not there, either," Freeman said. "My father went out of town and drove the car."

"Shows you what good ears I got," Fonzie said.

Silence again.

"I wouldn't mind knowing how to fix a car," Freeman said.

"It's a greasy job."

"I know that. But I'm kind of thinking about being an engineer and I guess there's more to things than wind resistance."

"Or a paint job," Fonzie said.

Freeman nodded agreement.

"No matter how good an engineer designs something, when it gets out on the job, sooner or later it breaks down," Fonzie said. "Somebody's got to fix it."

"I wonder where I could learn something about cars," Freeman said.

"I could show you some stuff."

"Hey, would you?"

"You want to see this game?" Fonzie asked.

"No. I don't care much for basketball."

"I don't either," Fonzie said. "You bounce the ball down the court and throw it in the basket and what've you got? You just got to turn around and bounce it down to the other end of the court and throw it in the other basket. You don't get nowhere."

"Why did you come to the game, then?"

"To yell."

"Me, too," Freeman said.

"I guess we might as well go in. After you."

Freeman started to open the door, then stopped.

"You almost tricked me again," he said. "You first."

"It's against my religion."

"Mine, too."

Fonzie sighed. "Well, if we're not going in," he said, "we might as well go over to the shop. I could show you a couple things. I've still got Cutter Margolin's rod over there that I borrowed to go to the station and get Mary Morning Glory."

"That's a *good* idea," Freeman said, excited.

"The only transportation I got is my bike. You'd have to ride on back."

"Great!"

"Let's go," Fonzie said. He gestured. "After you."

"Together," Freeman suggested.

Fonzie shrugged. "I guess my religion allows that," he said.

They walked toward the motorcycle.

"You know, it's just as well for the queen that I'm not showing up in there," Fonzie said. "When she yelled 'Hit that basket,' I was going to yell 'Hit the ref!' "

Freeman laughed. "You know why I came?" he said. "I was going to yell 'Z-Rah! for 'F-Rah!' "

"You're going to make a good mechanic," Fonzie told him.

EIGHT

Richie was standing in front of his dresser, inspecting his image in the mirror as he brushed his hair and scratched at a red spot at the tip of his nose. There was a knock at the door.

"Come in."

The door opened. Howard Cunningham looked in.

"It's me, the pretty good judge of people," he said.

"Hi, Dad. I'll be down to breakfast in a minute."

Howard entered. "That's not why I'm here," he said. "I ... uh ... I've been talking to your mother . . ." He sat down in Richie's chair. "There's something I want to talk to you about."

"Is she making you another one of those beef spread sandwiches with diced cucumbers? I told her you don't like them. Joanie told her, too."

"It's not that. I've learned that I'm not the good judge of people that I thought I was."

Richie shrugged. "You don't have to apologize for that." He put the brush down and faced his father. "See that red speck on my nose," he said. "Do you think that's anything?"

"It's a red speck."

"Like a disease, I mean."

Howard looked at him warily. "What kind of a disease?"

"How do I know? I'm not a doctor."

"You didn't have any particular disease in mind, then?"

Richie shook his head.

"It's not a disease," Howard told him. "It's a red speck."

"Good. I don't have to worry about that."

"Richie," Howard said, "the reason I'm here is: your mother told me about Fonzie wanting you to help him cheat on the history exam."

Richie peered at him, frowning. "How did she know about that?"

"Well, remember the night Fonzie was here? Joanie got a mild case of upset stomach and went to her room. Later, you and Fonzie came up here to your room. And Joanie's room is next to your room and—"

"She listened through the wall."

"Yes. She kept it to herself until this morning. "Which is a record, I guess, for Joanie for keeping a secret. Then, she told your mother and your mother told me and— And here I am."

"Things get around," Richie said.

"Is that what you were talking about—or, rather, talking around—the night of the wrestling matches?"

"Yeah."

"Richie, I don't know how you look at it," Howard said, "but if you think it would be Fonzie doing the cheating, but not you, you're wrong. You'd be doing it, too."

"I know that, Dad."

"Oh. Do you understand, too, that you

wouldn't really be doing him a favor? He'd be cheating himself, actually. Cheating himself out of knowledge that he ought to have."

"I know that, too, Dad."

"Uh-huh. Have you thought about the consequences? People *do* cheat and they *do* get away with it sometimes, but there's always a price to pay. A big price is in self-esteem. What you think about yourself is important, Richie. If you think of yourself as a cheater, pretty soon you get to the point where you don't like yourself. That can be disastrous."

Richie nodded. "I know that, Dad."

"What can I tell you, then, to keep you from doing this?"

"You don't have to tell me anything," Richie replied. "I already decided not to do it."

Howard sagged in the chair. "Why didn't you tell me that?"

"You didn't ask me, Dad."

"Oh . . ."

"I decided that night of the wrestling matches," Richie said.

"How has Fonzie reacted?"

"I haven't exactly told him yet," Richie said. "I tried to, but I caught him at a bad time. It was his privacy hour . . . or something like that . . ."

"He still doesn't know?"

Richie shook his head.

"When's the exam?" Howard asked.

"Today."

"Richie, you've got to tell him. You owe him that. He's expecting you to help him cheat."

"I'm going to tell him—first thing," Richie said.

"Well," Howard said, rising, "he seems like a nice kid . . . he'll understand."

"Oh, yeah, he'll understand," Richie said. "Then, after he understands, he'll kill me."

Howard paused at the door. "That's a definite drawback," he said.

From the other side of the wall came Joanie's voice. "I told you he was a hood!" she yelled.

Richie and his father looked at the wall.

"Do you know that your sister is really J. Edgar Hoover?" Howard said.

NINE

Fonzie arrived early at the school. Only a half-dozen-or-so students were on the grounds. He parked his motorcycle at the curb, then got a book, which was wrapped in plain brown paper, and the current issue of *Hot Rod* magazine from a saddlebag. Fonzie looked around to see how closely he was being observed. A boy on the school steps was watching him idly. Fonzie's eyes narrowed. The boy quickly looked away.

Confident that he had become all but invisible, Fonzie walked to a large tree and sat down at the base of it. He opened the magazine to the centerfold, then opened the book to a page that had been marked and placed it inside the magazine. Once more, he looked around, then, satisfied that he was not being spied upon, he raised the book and magazine and fixed his attention on the pages of the book. His eyes brightened with appreciation. Soon, the book had his full concentration.

After a time, Fonzie became aware of a presence. He glanced up. Polly was standing in front of him, her expression pained. Startled, Fonzie clapped the book and magazine closed and put them behind him.

"Fonzie, what've you got there?" Polly asked.

"*Hot Rod* magazine. You wouldn't like it. It's about hot rods."

"Inside the magazine, I mean."

100

"What do you mean inside?"

"You had something inside. I could see. The magazine isn't *that* thick."

"Sometimes they come out with special issues. Big, thick, lots of pages," Fonzie told her.

She gave up, looking depressed again.

"What's the matter?" Fonzie asked. "Drop a baton on your foot?"

She sighed. "Want me to sit down with you?"

"It's kind of dangerous," Fonzie said. "We might get a sudden thunder storm. This tree could get hit by lightning."

She giggled—but half-heartedly.

"How did you and Wanda Witherspoon make out?" Fonzie asked.

"Mary Motherwell."

"Whoever."

"Well . . . she says I'm the best cheerleader she's ever seen in a town this size."

Fonzie thought a moment. "Is that good or bad?"

"Just marvelous . . . I guess. . . ."

"Then, how come you're . . . uh. . . ?"

"To tell you the truth," Polly said, "I have reason to question Mary Motherwell's sincerity and honesty."

"What'd she do? Have her twirling fingers crossed when she said it?" Fonzie asked.

"No. But . . . well, as it turned out, she didn't come here just to watch me perform," Polly said. "She was also selling magazine subscriptions. She sold mother subscriptions to *Colliers* and *Saturday Evening Post* and *Life*."

"Well, maybe she figured as long as she was here. . . ."

"No, then she had Mother telephone everybody in town she knows and ask them to get subscriptions. And she told Mother what to say—how important taking the magazines was to my career."

"Well, as long as she liked your cheering. . . ," Fonzie said.

"I'm not even sure I can believe that. I asked her if she'd help me get into State, but I couldn't pin her down. All she would say was that I would probably be hearing from her."

"You will," Fonzie said. "I can almost guarantee it."

Polly brightened a bit. "Do you really think so?"

"Sure. She's not through selling your mother magazine subscriptions."

Polly sighed glumly again. "I just hate insincere people," she said. "They go around hurting other people. It's just terrible. I could *never* be that way."

"Sure you could," Fonzie said. "It's like twirling—it just takes practice."

"No. I'm just too naturally considerate of other people's feelings," she said. "I guess I get it from Mother."

"Yeah, you take after her, all right," Fonzie agreed.

"That's why I've decided to devote myself to *your* career instead of mine," Polly told him. "With me guiding you, Fonzie, you can become a really rich self-made man. First, of course, you've *got* to stop riding around on that motorcycle. And, I like the idea of you having a job after school, but not in that garage, Fonzie. You ought to work where you can meet a better class of people—people who can help you get ahead." She smiled. "We've got to make plans. We can talk about it when you come over to the house tonight."

"I'm not going to be in that vicinity," Fonzie told her.

"Oh. Well, tomorrow night, then."

"I'm not going to be in that vicinity tomorrow night, either."

"Oh. Well, I'm sure Freeman will, if you won't."

"Want to bet?" Fonzie said. "I'll give you odds."

Polly looked at him sadly. "Fonzie, I'm disappointed in you," she said. "I didn't think you could be so insincere."

"Could I interest you in a subscription to *Hot Rod?*" he asked.

"Oh!"

Polly turned and strode away.

Fonzie shrugged, then retrieved the book and magazine and fixed his attention once more on the book.

Again, he became aware of a presence. Looking up, he found Potsie standing in front of him.

"Hi," Potsie said amiably.

Fonzie remained silent.

"I was just going by," Potsie said.

"Don't let me stop you."

"And I saw you reading," Potsie said. "And I

was thinking . . . Fonzie . . . could I see that book after you finish with it?"

"What book?" Fonzie asked.

"The book you've got behind the magazine."

"Why would I be hiding a book behind my magazine?"

Potsie grinned. "You know. . . ."

"If I know, why am I asking you?"

"Uh . . . well. . . . Listen, Fonzie, come on—will you? I won't show it to anybody else. I'll just look at it, then I'll get it right back to you. I won't get fingerprints on it or anything. I promise."

"Okay," Fonzie said. "When I'm done with it, you can have it."

"Hey, great!" Potsie lowered his voice. "Is it really hot stuff?"

"Depends on how you look at it," Fonzie replied.

Potsie frowned. "What do you mean? You have to hold it in different ways or something?"

"I mean it depends on how your mind works," Fonzie told him. "Some guys could look at it and it'd be hot stuff. But other guys could look at it and it'd be boring. See what I mean?"

Potsie shook his head.

"You'll find out when I give it to you," Fonzie said. He looked past Potsie. Richie was approaching. "Hey, buddy!" he said.

Potsie turned. "Hi, Richie."

"Hi, Fonzie," Richie said, "I've got to talk to you."

The first bell rang.

"No time now," Fonzie said, rising. "Just

cough. You know what they say: one cough is worth a thousand words."

"That's 'one picture,'" Potsie said. He reached out. "Do I get the book now?"

"I'll let you know when you can have the book," Fonzie told him.

"Okay."

They walked toward the school building.

"This can't wait, Fonzie," Richie said. "It's about—" He glanced at Potsie. "It's about 'coughing,'" he told Fonzie.

"What's this about coughing?" Potsie asked.

The question went ignored.

"I've been thinking about it," Richie said to Fonzie, as they reached the steps. "Remember what you said about being friends? The thing is, when guys are really friends, one guy doesn't do something that will hurt the other guy."

"That's the way I see it," Fonzie replied. "Let's hear you cough."

They entered the building.

"I don't think you understand—" Richie began.

"Cough, Richie."

Richie made a feeble hacking sound.

"Hey, what's going on?" Potsie asked.

"What I'm trying to tell you is—" Richie said to Fonzie.

"Good morning, boys," a voice behind them said.

Looking back, they found Mrs. Wimper approaching them. Ralph was with her, a gloomy expression on his face.

"I hope we're ready for the exam," she said cheerily.

"We are," Fonzie told her. "How about you?"

"All prepared," she replied. "I warn you: the questions are not going to be easy. You'll need sharp minds as well as sharp pencils."

"Pointed heads, you mean?" Fonzie asked.

They had reached the entrance to the classroom.

"Fonzie, could you wait a minute?" Richie said.

"Richie," Mrs. Wimper said, "it's time for the bell."

"I've just got to talk to him a second."

The second bell rang.

"Now, see what you did," Mrs. Wimper said, "you made me late for my own class!" She made shooing motions. "Inside, boys."

They entered. Mrs. Wimper went to her desk, and Richie and Fonzie and Potsie and Ralph made their way along the aisles toward their seats. The other students were already in their places.

"I can't do it!" Richie whispered quickly to Fonzie.

"Don't worry about it," Fonzie told him. "It's not a great cough, but it's a good enough cough. It's the numbers that count. One for false, two for true."

"That's what I mean. I can't—"

"Richard!" Mrs. Wimper said from the front of the room. "If you don't mind . . ."

"Yes, mam," he replied, taking his seat.

Fonzie, already seated, put his book with the plain paper wrapping and magazine under his desk.

"This will be a true or false test," Mrs. Wimper

said, addressing the class. "I hope you all understand how important it is. It covers most of our
work. And, by your grades, I will know how much
you have learned." She began handing out sheafs
of papers to the students seated at the front of
the rows. "Pass these back, please."

Richie whispered hoarsely. "Fonzie—"

"Richard!" Mrs. Wimper said sharply. "You're
disturbing the class. Please put a tick-a-lock on
your lips!"

"Yes, ma'm," he replied drearily.

Mrs. Wimper stood at the front of the classroom. When the test papers had been passed out,
she addressed the students again.

"As we sow, so shall we reap," she said. "The
studying that you have sown will determine the
grade that you reap. Now, are there any questions
before we begin?"

Silence.

"Very well. No more talking. Now . . . begin."

The students lowered their eyes to their papers.

Mrs. Wimper went to her desk and sat down
and became busy, making up the homework
schedule for the following week.

Fonzie coughed.

There was no response from Richie, who was
concentrating fully on the test.

Fonzie coughed again.

As before, Richie ignored the sound.

Fonzie hacked loudly.

All around the classroom, heads raised. Eyes focused on Fonzie.

Fonzie looked toward the front of the room. Mrs. Wimper was peering at him. "I guess I got a cold," he said. "I must've caught a germ from biology."

Mrs. Wimper touched a finger to her lips. "Shh-shh-shh!"

The students returned their attention to the test. For a few moments there was quiet. Then Fonzie whistled softly.

Richie kept his eyes on the test paper. Perspiration broke out on his forehead.

Fonzie whistled again, louder.

"Fonzie, is that you?" Mrs. Wimper asked.

The other students looked up again.

"Is what me?" Fonzie asked innocently.

"That whistling."

"Did I whistle?"

"I'm afraid you did."

He looked at Richie. "She says I whistled," he told him. "Did you hear me whistle?"

Before Richie could reply, Mrs. Wimper spoke again. "It doesn't matter whether Richard heard you," she said. "*I* heard you. I want to know the meaning of it."

"I do it absent-minded," Fonzie told her. "When I'm working, you know, hard, and thinking, sometimes I start whistling to myself."

"Oh . . . yes, I see. . . . Well, please, don't do it again."

"Yeah," Fonzie replied, nodding.

"Back to work, class!"

Once more, the students concentrated on the test.

For a few minutes, all was quiet. Then the door opened and a student entered and went to Mrs. Wimper's desk and began whispering to her. Mrs. Wimper nodded. Then the student departed.

Mrs. Wimper rapped on her desk with a ruler.

The students raised their eyes to her.

"I have to go to the main office," she told them. "But I want you to continue the test just as if I were here. I'm going to put you on your honor," she said, getting up. "I know you won't disappoint me. And, to make sure that you don't . . . Polly," she said, "I want you to report any instances of cheating."

"Yes, ma'm!" Polly said exuberantly.

"I'm sure I can count on you," Mrs. Wimper said, going to the door.

"I'll take names!" Polly told her.

Mrs. Wimper departed.

Fonzie immediately turned to Richie. "Are you deaf?" he asked.

"Is that a question on the test?" Polly demanded. "Are you cheating?"

"Fonzie, I can't do it," Richie said. "I wouldn't be your friend if I did."

Fonzie gestured off-handedly. "I knew it," he said. "I said to myself, 'He won't come through.' "

"What are you talking about?" Polly said. "Is it about cheating?"

Fonzie turned to Freeman Locke. "Hey, have you got that thing?" he said.

Freeman handed him a folded piece of paper.

Richie realized immediately what was happening. Fonzie, not sure that he could count on

Richie, had also made an arrangement with Freeman Locke.

"Cheating!" Polly said to Fonzie. "You got the answers from Freeman! I'm going to tell!"

"Mary Motherwell," Fonzie said to her.

"What?"

"How'd you like everybody in school to know how come your mother started taking *Colliers* and *Saturday Evening Post* and *Life?*"

Polly went pale.

"Fonzie," Richie begged, "don't look at that paper. It won't help you. Not really, it won't."

Fonzie looked at the folded piece of paper, then at Richie. "You must be nuts," he said. "I couldn't do anything without this."

"What I'm saying is, in the long run—"

"Listen, will you let me do my test?" Fonzie said. "About that other—I'll see you later."

"But, Fonzie—"

The door opened.

All eyes returned to the papers.

Mrs. Wimper entered. "Well, Polly?" she said, going to her desk.

Polly swallowed hard. "Nothing to report," she said weakly.

"Wonderful! I knew you students could be trusted!" She sat down at her desk again. "Carry on!"

When the room became quiet again, Richie leaned toward Fonzie's desk, trying to see if he was copying the answers from the paper that he had received from Freeman Locke.

Fonzie looked across at him. "What're you trying to do, Cunningham—cheat?" he said.

Richie quickly pulled back.

"Shhh!" Mrs. Wimper said.

A few minutes later, the bell rang, ending the period.

"Leave your test papers on my desk," Mrs. Wimper called out. "I'll grade them this evening. Tomorrow, we'll find out how we all did. Good luck!"

Fonzie got his book and magazine from under his seat, then rose, taking his test paper with him, and left. He did not look at Richie.

"What was going on?" Potsie asked Richie.

"Nothing."

"What was that coughing and whistling? Was that signals? Hey! Fonzie wanted you to tell him the answers, didn't he? That's what he meant when he said two for false and one for true."

"The other way around, one for false and two for true," Richie said.

They headed for the front of the room with their papers.

"But you didn't do it," Potsie said.

Richie nodded. "I didn't do it. I couldn't."

They reached the teacher's desk and dropped their test papers on it and moved on toward the exit.

"He's going to kill you," Potsie told Richie.

"Boy, I know it."

"He's waiting for you outside the door," Potsie said. "He's going to kill you dead."

Richie halted.

"You can't stay here the rest of your life," Potsie said.

Richie started toward the door again, then halted once more. "He wouldn't hit me in school, would he?" he said.

"Why not?"

Richie thought. "You're right," he decided, "why not?"

Mrs. Wimper spoke to them. "Boys, you're going to be late for your next class."

"We're waiting for you," Richie said.

"For me?" she asked puzzledly.

"If you're going somewhere, we thought we'd walk with you," Richie said.

"For protection," Potsie explained.

"Why would I need protection?"

"Not your protection, Richie's protection," Potsie said. "You see, Fonzie—"

"Potsie's joking," Richie told Mrs. Wimper, breaking in. "We just thought you might be going back to the main office or somewhere."

She shook her head. "No. This is my classroom, this is where I'm staying. Now, go on. You'll be late if you don't."

Richie and Potsie advanced toward the door.

"Maybe he'll hit you a glancing blow and you'll only lose a couple teeth," Potsie said.

"Boy, thanks, that makes me feel a lot better."

They reached the door and halted again.

"You look," Richie said.

Potsie leaned forward and peeked out into the corridor. "He's gone," he reported to Richie.

"Are you *sure*?"

"Almost everybody's gone," Potsie told him. "They're all in class already."

From behind them came Mrs. Wimper's voice. "Boys!"

Richie and Potsie hustled from the room. When they were in the hall, Richie quickly looked both ways. As Potsie had reported, Fonzie was nowhere in sight.

"You didn't have anything to worry about," Potsie said.

"Listen, Fonzie asked me to help him cheat and I told him I would, and then, when we got in class, I didn't," Richie said. "Is he going to let me get away with that?"

Potsie shook his head. "He's going to kill you, all right."

They walked along the corridor in the direction of their next class.

"He's going to get me after school," Richie said.

"If not before."

"What can I do?"

"Only one thing, Richie."

"I guess you're right. Face up to it."

"No, change your name and move to Argentina," Potsie said. "If you face up to it, the way Fonzie is going to wham you, you won't have a face left to ever face up to anything else again."

"I've got it coming, I guess," Richie said.

"Yeah, anybody who's dumb enough to double-cross Fonzie deserves what he gets."

"I didn't mean to double-cross him," Richie protested. "I tried to tell him I couldn't help him cheat, but he wouldn't listen."

"Maybe he'll take that into consideration and only break one of your legs," Potsie said.

The bell rang.

At the same instant, Richie and Potsie darted into their next classroom.

The teacher, Mrs. Corboy, eyed them coolly. "You're late," she told them.

"I thought it was a tie," Richie said.

"Wasn't that bell a little early?" Potsie said.

"Never mind the excuses, just take your seats."

They moved down the aisle.

"Even if it *does* look like a double-cross, I did what was right," Richie whispered to Potsie.

"Nathan Hale thought he was right, too," Potsie said. "But they hung him."

"This is different."

"Yeah . . . Fonzie won't hang you. . . ."

Mrs. Corboy spoke to them again. "Just take your seats, please, don't carry on a discussion."

They sat down.

"Let's all open our books to the chapter on adverbs," Mrs. Corboy said, addressing the class.

Potsie whispered to Richie again. "Listen, Rich, we're pals. If you decide to face up to Fonzie and you want me along with you, just say the word."

"Thanks Potsie. I'd appreciate that."

Potsie's face fell. "Some friend," he said. "You want me to get my face pushed in, too? Who'll nurse you back to health?"

"Okay then, *don't* come with me," Richie said.

"Now you're talking sense," Potsie whispered. "But don't ever forget that I offered to go with you."

"Thanks."

"I'll be with you in spirit," Potsie said.

Once more, Mrs. Corboy spoke to them. "If you boys are finished," she said, "do you mind if we begin the lesson?"

"That's what we were talking about—the lesson," Potsie said.

"Oh? Fine. Perhaps then, you'll define the adverb for us."

"Adverb?"

"That's the lesson," Mrs. Corboy said.

"You want to know what it is?"

She nodded.

Potsie cogitated for a moment. "Let me put it this way," Potsie said. "An adverb is— An adverb is sort of a—"

"Yes?"

"An adverb," Potsie said, "is a word that's not a noun and not a verb and not an adjective and not a conjunction . . ."

"You're not telling us what an adverb *is*."

"I'm getting to that," Potsie said. "After you find the nouns and verb and adjectives and conjunction, an adverb is—"

The whole class—and the teacher—leaned slightly toward him.

"—is what's left over," Potsie said.

The whole class, as one person, groaned.

"I think I'd like to have you drop in after school," Mrs. Corboy said to Potsie. "You and I can discuss adverbs for a while."

Potsie sagged.

Richie's hand went up.

"Yes, Richard?"

"I don't know what an adverb is, either, Mrs. Corboy."

She seemed surprised. "Richard, I'm sure you do."

"I forgot," he told her.

"Very well. I'll expect to see *you* after school, too." She looked around the room. "Anyone else who wants to confess?"

Silence.

"All right. Now, let's get to work."

Potsie whispered to Richie. "What'd you do that for?"

"Fonzie can't get me if I'm in here staying after school," Richie explained.

"Smart!"

"If I can get kept after in the rest of my classes today, I may not have to leave the school for a week," Richie said.

"You're just putting it off."

"I know."

"Sooner or later, he's going to kill you."

"I know," Richie moaned.

"But, look at the bright side," Potsie said.

"What's the bright side?"

"Nobody'll be able to say you died without knowing what an adverb is."

TEN

When Richie and Potsie reported to Mrs. Corboy's classroom after school, she was completing her daily records.

"I'll be with you in just a second, boys," she said.

"Don't hurry," Richie replied, as he and Potsie took seats in the first row. "We came for a long stay. We really want to get straightened out on adverbs."

Mrs. Corboy looked at him narrowly. "Your interest in adverbs is commendable," she said. "I sort of have the feeling, however, that there's more to it than that."

"Sure," Richie said. "If you want to straighten us out on verbs—or *anything*—we've got the time for that, too."

"How about adnouns," Potsie suggested.

"There's no such thing."

"We can invent them," Potsie said. "And you can take all the credit. You could go down in English history as the inventor of the adnoun."

"I think I'll be able to resist that opportunity," she said. Then she returned her attention to the records.

"Have you heard anything?" Richie asked Potsie, keeping his voice low.

"About what?"

"About Fonzie!"

Potsie shook his head. "Maybe he isn't going to do anything."

"He told me he'd see me later. You know what that means."

"Yeah, he's going to—"

"Don't say that!" Richie broke in.

"All right, boys," Mrs. Corboy said, putting the records aside. "Now . . . adverbs. If you were paying attention in class today, I'm sure that by now you know what an adverb is." She focused on Potsie. "Would you like to try that definition again?" she asked.

"An adverb is . . . a word. . . ."

She motioned, encouraging him. "Yes, yes. . . ."

". . . a word that . . . uh . . . adds meaning to the verb?"

Mrs. Corboy beamed. "You know!"

"Was that right?" Potsie asked, grinning.

"Yes. Perfect. Now, give me an example."

Potsie's grin faded. "Oh. That's a little tougher."

"An adverb for the verb 'ran,' " Mrs. Corboy suggested.

"Ran?"

She nodded.

"Ran where?"

"It doesn't make any difference."

"It probably does to the guy who's running," Potsie said. "Suppose he's running into the lake and he can't swim?"

"Please . . . don't confuse the issue," Mrs. Corboy said. "Just give me an adverb for the verb 'ran.' "

"Could you give me a hint?"

"All right. Finish this sentence: The boy ran—How did he run?"

"Into the lake."

"That's where he ran. I want to know how he ran."

"Oh!" Potsie said. "The boy ran like a shot. Okay?"

Mrs. Corboy sighed. "No, not okay. 'Like a shot' is a phrase. I want a word that tells me how the boy ran."

"Down," Potsie said.

"What?"

"He ran down," Potsy said.

"We're talking about a boy, not a clock. Try again."

"The boy ran— Uh, let's see." Potsie turned to Richie. "How's the time?"

"Keep it up," Richie said.

"The boy ran—"

"Are you boys late for something?" Mrs. Corboy asked.

"Yeah. But we want to be," Potsie said.

She blinked at him.

"The boy ran— Uh, the boy ran, uh—"

"*Slowly!*" Mrs. Corboy said, breaking.

"Oh, slowly," Potsie said. "I see the problem now, I was thinking of another boy. He runs fast."

"The adverb is slowly," Mrs. Corboy said. "Do you understand? It adds meaning to the verb 'ran.' Is that clear?"

"Sure," Potsie replied. "He was in no hurry to

get into the lake. I don't blame him, if he couldn't swim."

"Richie," Mrs. Corboy said, "do you think you know what an adverb is now?"

"Potsie just confused me," Richie said. "I need more study on it. Maybe I could just sit here for a couple hours—"

"Richie, you know what an adverb is," the teacher said, interrupting. "After this morning's class, I checked some of your old papers. You've known what an adverb is—and how to use it—for quite some time."

"I probably forgot," Richie said.

"How could you possibly forget a thing like that?"

Richie thought for a moment. "Amnesia?" he suggested.

She shook her head. "You boys are using me," she said. "I don't know what it's about. I don't think I want to know. But the game is over. You're dismissed."

Richie and Potsie sat motionless.

"Goodbye, boys," Mrs. Corboy said.

Reluctantly, they rose, then moved slowly toward the doorway.

Richie halted. "Maybe I could clean up the room for you," he said to the teacher.

"The custodians do that, Richard."

They proceeded. At the doorway, they halted and Potsie looked out.

"All clear," he reported to Richie.

They left the room and walked cautiously toward the main exit.

"You know, maybe you're worried for nothing," Potsie said. "Fonzie's had all day to think about it. He's probably changed his mind."

Richie looked doubtful.

"He probably realizes by now that you were right, not helping him cheat," Potsie said. "He's probably laughing about the whole thing. Don't you think?"

Richie shook his head.

"Then where is he?" Potsie said. He indicated the empty corridor. "Look. Everybody's gone. He'd be hanging around, wouldn't he, if he was after you?"

"He's outside," Richie said.

Potsie nodded. "I bet you're right. He's out there waiting. He's really going to kill you."

"We shouldn't have stayed after school," Richie said. "If we'd have gone home when everybody else did, maybe we could have got lost in the crowd. Now, the second we step out the door, he'll see me."

"Here's an idea," Potsie said. "Grab your leg and start yelling."

Richie halted, looking at him baffledly. "How will that help?"

"We'll say you broke your leg," Potsie said. "Then we'll call an ambulance and they'll back up to the door and take you out on a stretcher."

Richie moved on. "Thanks," he said sourly.

"It's an idea."

Nearing the doors, they approached them warily.

"You go ahead and look out," Richie said.

Potsie proceeded. At the doors, he stopped and looked out onto the school yard.

"See anybody?" Richie called.

"I see Ralph."

"What's he doing?"

"Sitting on the steps."

"What about Fonzie?"

"Why would Ralph be sitting on Fonzie?" Potsie asked.

"Cut it out! Do you see Fonzie?"

"He's not out there."

Richie joined him. He, too, looked out onto the school yard.

"You're right, he's not there," Richie said.

"See, I told you, he's probably forgotten about the whole thing."

"Maybe so," Richie said hopefully.

"Sure," Potsie said. "Fonzie likes you. He wouldn't kill you for a little thing like making him flunk a history test."

"Right," Richie said. "Like you said, he's had the whole day to think about it, and he's probably laughing about it by now."

"If he even remembers it," Potsie said. "Let's go."

They went out.

Ralph immediately jumped up. "Hey, where've you been?" he asked Richie. "Fonzie's looking for you."

Richie whipped around and ran back into the school building.

"What did I say?" Ralph asked Potsie.

"The magic words," Potsie told him. "Did Fonzie tell you *why* he wants to see Richie?"

"No."

"To kill him," Potsie said. "Richie was supposed to help Fonzie cheat on the history test, but, at the last minute, he couldn't do it. So Fonzie's going to flunk."

"That explains it," Ralph said. "Fonzie was asking everybody where Richie was. I couldn't figure out why he wanted to see him so bad."

"Badly," Potsie said. "That's an adverb."

"What?"

"Forget it."

They went to the door.

"Fonzie's not here now," Ralph told Richie. "He hung around a long time, until everybody had gone, then he went, too." He looked grim. "Boy, he really wants to see you," he told Richie.

"If it was just seeing, I wouldn't mind. It's what comes after that bothers me."

"You've got to hide out," Potsie said.

"Where?"

"If you've been thinking about taking a world cruise, now's the time," Ralph told him.

"No, the place to hide out is where nobody would ever expect you to hide out," Potsie said. "I read that in a detective story. There was this crook, and the cops were after him, so what he did was, he parked his car in front of the police station and sat in it all day."

"That's dumb," Ralph said.

"No, it's smart. That was the last place the

cops thought to look for him, right in front of the police station."

"Did he get away?" Richie asked.

Potsie shook his head. "He got arrested for illegal parking. But the idea was good."

"What's Richie supposed to do, go stand in front of the police station?" Ralph asked.

"No. Put yourself in Fonzie's place. He's looking for Richie, right? Where wouldn't he expect him to be?"

"I already suggested that—on a world cruise," Ralph said.

"Let me put it another way. Where does Richie usually go right after school?"

"Arnold's."

"Right. Now, Fonzie knows that. And Fonzie also knows that, by now, Richie knows that Fonzie is looking for him. So, what's Fonzie thinking? He's thinking that the one place that Richie *won't* be is Arnold's."

"Why not?"

"Because Fonzie knows that Richie knows that Fonzie knows that— Take my word for it," Potsie said. He turned to Richie. "Go to Arnold's and sit in a booth and you'll be safe," he said. "Because that's the one place Fonzie won't look for you."

"It does make sense, kind of," Richie said. "Okay."

They left the school and headed in the direction of the drive-in.

"This isn't going to work," Ralph said. "Fonzie will be waiting at Arnold's—and Pow!"

"It *will* work," Potsie insisted. "Right now,

Fonzie is out looking in all the places where he thinks Richie would go to hide. Like a movie. Or in his attic at home. Or in a sewer. Or—"

"Are you telling me that Fonzie is looking in the sewers?"

"If he's already looked in the movies and in Richie's attic, he is," Potsie said.

From behind them came the sound of a motorcycle.

"Hide me!" Richie said.

Potsie and Ralph surrounded him—as much as they could. That still left a great deal of Richie showing.

The sound of the motorcycle grew louder.

"False alarm," Ralph said.

Richie peeked out. A motorcycle was going by. But Fonzie was not aboard it.

"This is no way to live," Richie said, as they moved on. "Did you see me? I almost jumped out of my skin. How long can I keep this up?"

"Until Fonzie gets tired of chasing you," Potsie said. "Richie, do it my way, will you? Believe me, I know what I'm doing. I've read more detective stories than you have."

"You know how this is going to end?" Ralph said to Richie. "You're going to get arrested for illegal parking."

They were nearing the drive-in.

"Was I right or was I right?" Potsie said triumphantly. "He's not here."

"How do you know?"

"Do you see his bike? If his bike isn't here, Fonzie's not here."

"I guess that's right," Ralph said.

Richie relaxed a bit. "Maybe your idea isn't so bad," he said to Potsie.

"Badly," Ralph told him. "That's an adverb."

Richie ignored the attempt to correct his grammar. "Usually," he said to Potsie, "if you want to find Fonzie along around this time of day, here is where you look. But, you're right—no bike, no Fonzie."

"Didn't I tell you? He's in a sewer somewhere."

They entered Arnold's. It was crowded. As they made their way toward the booths, Marsha, the waitress, came toward them.

"Fonzie's looking for you, Richie," she said.

Richie started to bolt. But Potsie and Ralph grabbed him and held him.

"Is he here?" Potsie asked Marsha.

She halted and looked at Potsie warily. "What do you mean, is he here? Of course he's here. You've got hold of him."

"No, is *Fonzie* here?"

She shook her head. "He was here but he left," she said, going on.

"It's safe," Potsie told Richie.

"No it isn't! Your idea is crazy. He shouldn't have been here at all."

"There's nothing wrong with my idea," Potsie protested. "Fonzie just isn't doing it right. But he's learning. He's gone, isn't he? And why is he gone? Because he's figured it out. He's looking where he thinks you'll be—in the movies, in your attic, in the sewers. You're safe here."

They moved on through the crowd, then joined Trudy and Sandy in a booth.

"Fonzie's looking for you, Richie," Trudy said.

"I know."

"He's been asking everybody where you are," Sandy said. "What does he want?"

"Didn't he say?"

Sandy shook her head. "I asked him. But he just looked at me. You know how Fonzie can look at you."

Richie shuddered. "I know."

"What's going on?" Trudy said. "What's so mysterious?"

"Fonzie's going to kill him," Potsie told her.

"Oh." Trudy turned to Sandy. "Let's dance," she said.

They left the booth and joined the other kids who were moving animatedly to the music from the juke box.

"That's sympathy," Ralph said.

Marsha, the waitress, stopped at the booth. "What'll it be?" she asked.

"Do you have any quick poison?" Richie asked glumly.

"It's all poison, Richie," she said. "But it's slow."

"Slowly," Ralph told her. "That's an adverb."

"Oh, Richie—" Marsha said. "If you're looking for Fonzie, he's back. He just rode up."

"He's not supposed to do that," Potsie said. "Right now, he's supposed to be in the sewers."

Richie was scrambling up. "I'm not here!" he told Marsha.

"The way you're acting, you're not all there, either," she said, getting out of his way.

"Out through the kitchen!" Potsie said to Richie, sliding from the booth.

Richie, Potsie and Ralph ran to the rear of the drive-in and pushed through a pair of swinging doors, racing into the kitchen.

"Nobody allowed!" the cook yelled at them.

"We're leaving!" Potsie told him.

They dashed through the rear exit and ran across the parking area—and found themselves face to face with a tall fence.

"Over!" Ralph said.

Potsie and Ralph made a sling of their hands and Richie put a foot in it and boosted himself up and over the fence.

"Wait for us!" Potsie called after him.

"I'm going home!" Richie shouted back.

"Fonzie'll kill us!" Ralph said.

"He's after me, not you!"

"Oh, yeah—that's right."

Richie hurried through the back yard he had landed in. When he reached the street, he began running again. But after he had gone a few blocks, he slowed to a trot, then, finally, winded, lapsed into a weary walk. Continuing, he kept looking back, expecting to see Fonzie coming after him. Fonzie did not appear, however. Eventually, Richie reached the Cunningham house.

Joanie was lying across a living room chair, reading a book which was open on the floor. "That hood was here looking for you," she told her brother.

"How long ago?"

"I don't know."

"How can you know he was here but not know how long ago?" Richie asked.

"Mom told me."

"Oh."

Richie walked on to the kitchen.

"Your friend Fonzie stopped by," Marion told him. "I told him you were probably at Arnold's."

"Did he tell you why he stopped?" Richie asked.

"No."

"Did he say anything about the attic?"

Marion looked at him curiously. "What about the attic?"

"Nothing," Richie replied, opening the refrigerator. "I just thought he might have said something about it."

"Why would he?"

"Just making conversation maybe," Richie said, getting makings for a sandwich from the refrigerator.

"Richie, don't spoil your dinner."

"I just want a snack."

"A sandwich is too much," his mother said. "Have a grape."

He put the sandwich material back. "How about a piece of pie?"

"Well...."

Richie took the pie from the refrigerator and put it on the table, then got a knife from a drawer.

"How did he seem?" Richie asked, cutting a large slice of pie.

"You're going to ruin your dinner with a big slice like that," Marion said. "How did who seem?"

"Fonzie."

Marion pondered the question. "Greasy," she replied.

"That's how he looked. He was probably at the garage," Richie said. "How did he act, though?"

"Very gentlemanly," Marion said. "He complimented me on my mashed potatoes again." She frowned. "He did seem anxious to see you, though."

"Boy, I bet."

"Is something wrong, Richie?"

"What could be wrong?"

"Today, in school, you— Uh, you didn't—"

Richie shook his head. "I didn't," he told her.

"I was sure you wouldn't. I'm glad Fonzie took it so well," she said. "I'm sure he realized that it was for his own best good. Cheaters, you know, Richie, never win."

Richie thought for a second. "How do you know?" he asked.

"Pardon?"

"How do you know that cheaters never win?" he asked. "If they cheat and get away with it, then nobody knows about it, and they win, don't they?"

"Not really," his mother replied, beginning to peel one of the potatoes that she had placed on the counter. "It's on their conscience."

"How do you know?"

"Because my mother told me so, the same way I'm telling you," Marion replied.

"But what if it *doesn't* bother their conscience? What if they think cheating is okay—even right—and, the way they look at it, cheating is smart, not bad?"

Marion looked at him sternly. "What are they teaching you at that school?"

"I didn't learn that in school, I just figured it out myself."

"Ask your father," she said, turning her attention to the potatoes again. "He understands questions like that."

"What I'm asking is—"

"Have some more pie," Marion said.

"Okay." Richie picked up the knife. Then, suddenly, he cocked an ear. "Do you hear that?"

His mother listened. "What?"

"Isn't that a motorcycle?"

"Oh, that. Yes, I think it is. It's probably your friend again."

Richie had dropped the knife and was running for the back door.

"Richard! Where are you going?"

"The North Pole!" he called back.

"Be home for dinner!"

It was dark when Richie returned to the Cunningham house. He opened the front door quietly. From the living room came the sound of the TV. Richie walked softly toward the stairs.

"I think that's him," he heard his father say.

Richie started up the steps. But he was not fast enough. Howard Cunningham appeared in the opening to the living room.

"Hi, Dad," Richie said offhandedly.

Howard studied him, silent.

"I was just going up to my room," Richie said.

"Did you have dinner somewhere?"

"No."

"Aren't you hungry?"

"I guess I am," Richie replied. "I haven't thought about it much."

Marion Cunningham appeared from the living room. "Richard, *where* have you been?" she demanded.

"At the library."

Howard shook his head. "The one place we didn't think to look," he said. "We called your friends, we called the North Pole—"

"I'm sorry about that, Dad," Richie said. "I didn't know where I was going when I left. So, I just said— I'm sorry."

"I'll warm up your dinner for you," Marion said, heading for the kitchen.

"Mom—"

"Let her," Howard said to him. "That is, if you can hang around long enough to eat."

"Sure."

"Want to come in the living room and wait?"

"All right."

In the living room, Howard switched off the television set. "You had us a little worried," he said to Richie. "As I told you, we called all your friends. None of them knew where you were."

"They've got a private room at the library where you can take books to do research," Richie said, sitting down on the sofa.

"What were you researching?"

Richie frowned. "Gee, I don't remember."

"Potsie called back a short while ago," Howard said. "That was after I called him earlier to ask him if he knew where you were. When he telephoned me, he told me about your problem with Fonzie."

"That's why I went to the library," Richie said. "I figured that was the one place in town where Fonzie wouldn't go."

"What next?" Howard asked, settling in his chair.

"I'm not sure. But, I was thinking. . . You know what might be good for me? Working on a ranch somewhere out West."

"Are you in bad health or something?"

"Not now. But I plan to be."

"I see. Richie, when I was about your age, I knew a man who was convinced that the world was going to come to an end in 1934. August, '34, to be exact. At 3:17 in the afternoon. The only thing he wasn't absolutely positive about was the exact day in August."

"Yeah. . . ?" Richie said, puzzled.

"It didn't happen," Howard said.

Richie smiled faintly. "I kind of figured it didn't."

"But, even if it had, that man wouldn't have been there to see it," Howard said. "He died in '32. The doctor said he worried himself to death."

Richie frowned. "Can you do that?"

"Yes. But, the point is: this man worried himself to death about something that never happened. A lot of people do that, Richie. Their fear of a catastrophe is bigger than the catastrophe itself."

"It doesn't fit this case, though," Richie told him. "Fonzie is really going to kill me."

Howard shook his head. "He isn't going to kill you."

"Yes, he is. He's been tracking me all over town."

"I know. But listen to what you're saying. You're saying he's going to *kill* you. He isn't going to kill you, Richie. You're scaring yourself to death with that word."

Richie was silent for a moment, thinking. "I guess he isn't going to really *kill* me," he conceded. "But he's going to pop me one—and really good."

"Hit you, you mean?"

Richie nodded.

"Have you ever been hit before?"

"Yeah. It hurts."

"When you were hit before—did you survive?"

"I'm here."

"After Fonzie hits you, do you think you'll still be here?" Howard asked.

"Yes."

"Then it isn't going to be as bad as your imagination has told you it will."

"I guess not," Richie said. "But . . . I still don't want to get hit."

"I don't blame you for that," his father said. "You, uh ... you could fight back, though, instead of running away."

Richie shook his head. "Fonzie knows how to handle himself," he said. "I saw him mad once. A guy in a motorcycle gang was riding him. He was saying things, trying to get Fonzie to fight, because he was bigger than Fonzie." Richie winced, recalling. "Fonzie really cut him up. With his fists."

"That's not good," Howard said. "We could go to the police about it."

"No, I'd rather not. What are the police going to do? Give me a permanent bodyguard?"

"Has Fonzie threatened you?"

"He hasn't said anything, if that's what you mean. But, he won't. He didn't say anything to that gang guy, either. He just plowed into him."

"If he hasn't threatened you, Richie, maybe you're all wrong about this."

"He's been trailing me all over town. He's never done that before. Why is he doing it now—if he doesn't plan on kil— On konking me."

"It *could* be something else."

"What?"

"Maybe he wants another invitation to dinner. He really liked your mother's mashed potatoes," Howard said.

Richie shook his head. "Anyway, I guess I've got it coming," he said. "When he first asked me to help him cheat, I should have told him no right then. But I didn't. I put it off. And I put it off too long. He went into class expecting me to help him—and *that's* when I told him."

"That wasn't exactly fair," Howard agreed. "But it wasn't fair for him to ask you to cheat, either." —

"Dad, it's done. Now there isn't anything I can do about it."

"Except run away?"

"Sooner or later, he'll catch me."

"And, in the meantime, you're going to worry yourself to death about what's going to happen when he *does* catch up with you. Richie, why put yourself through that? Face him. Get it over with."

"I guess I might as well," Richie said. "I'm getting tired of hiding out."

"I'm sure it won't be as bad as you think it will."

"Maybe . . ."

Marion reappeared. "You dinner is ready, dear," she said to Richie.

Richie got up. At that same instant, the sound of a motorcycle came from outside.

"Speak of the Devil," Howard said.

Richie ran to the stairs and raced up the steps.

"You're forgetting!" Howard called after him. "You're going to face him!"

Richie was gone.

There was a knock at the door.

"Don't open it!" Marion said to her husband, panicking. "I'll turn off the lights and he'll think we're not home."

"It's too late for that, Marion."

Howard opened the door. Fonzie was there.

"Hey . . ." Fonzie said amiably.

"Don't you dare lay a finger on that boy!" Marion said to him from behind her husband.

Fonzie peered at Howard. "You let your wife call you 'boy?'" he asked.

"I don't think she meant me."

Fonzie shrugged. "Is Richie around?"

"I suppose that depends on your definition of 'around,'" Howard replied. "He ... uh ... he was at the library earlier."

"Oh. Is that where he is?"

"Well, it's hard to say—"

"Assault and battery is against the law, you know!" Marion told Fonzie.

He stared at her, perplexed.

"Marion has a legal mind," Howard told him. "Things like that just pop out."

"Oh. You say Richie's at the library?"

"Let me put it this way," Howard replied. "Technically, I didn't exactly say that he isn't at the library."

"You mean you don't know where he is?"

"In what specific, exact spot? No, I don't know what specific, exact spot he's in."

"I been chasing him around ever since school let out," Fonzie said.

"Oh? Any particular reason?"

"I got something to settle with him," Fonzie told him. "It's private."

Howard sighed. "I was afraid of that."

"Huh?"

"Well, if you see him, tell him his mother and I still live here," Howard said.

"Violence never solved anything!" Marion told Fonzie.

He peered at her again. "You're kind of a crazy lady," He said. "But I guess your mashed potatoes make up for it." He nodded to Howard and Marion. "Tell Richie I'm looking for him. Tell him I'll see him tomorrow."

"Not if he sees you first—if history repeats itself," Howard said.

Fonzie looked at them both again in a baffled way, then, shaking his head, departed.

Howard closed the door.

From outside came the sound of a motorcycle. After a moment, the sound faded.

"Richie!" Howard called. "You can come out now!"

"Oh, my!" Marion said fretfully. "I'm sure his dinner is cold again by now." She set out for the kitchen.

Howard called out again. "Richieeee! All clear!"

Richie still did not appear.

Howard started up the stairs. But at that moment, Richie came into view at the top of the steps.

"Where were you?" Howard asked.

"In the attic."

"Why did you go all the way up there?"

"It's as far away as I could get," Richie replied, descending the stairs. "What did Fonzie say?"

"He has something to settle with you."

"Oh, boy!"

"I take back what I said before," Howard told him. "It may be as bad as you think it is."

Richie reached the main floor and they walked toward the kitchen.

"But, you still have to face it," Howard said. "You can't take the attic to school with you."

"I know."

"He said he'd see you tomorrow."

"If there was just some way to stop the earth from turning . . . ," Richie said thoughtfully.

They reached the kitchen.

"Howard . . . I was just thinking. . . ," Marion said. "I know it would be wrong . . . and, normally, I wouldn't even suggest it. But . . . do you think Fonzie could be bribed?"

"With what?"

"Well . . . if I made up a big batch of stiff, lumpy mashed potatoes. . . ."

ELEVEN

Determined to face up to Fonzie, Richie arrived at school early the next morning. He scouted the grounds, looking for a grassy spot. When he found it, he took his stand, knowing that at least he had a soft place to fall after Fonzie hit him.

Soon, the other students began arriving. Before long, the grounds were crowded. Richie kept listening for the sound of a motorcycle, growing increasingly apprehensive. His palms were moist. Every once in a while, he had to draw perspiration from his forehead.

Potsie was the first to approach him. "What's the matter with you? Are you crazy?" Potsie said. "You're standing right out here in plain sight."

"I'm going to get it over with," Richie said.

"You *are* crazy!"

"It's the only way," Richie said. "I can't keep running. Sooner or later, Fonzie's going to catch me."

"What's the matter with later?" Potsie asked.

Ralph arrived. "What're you doing standing right out here in the middle of everything?" he said to Richie.

"He's crazy," Potsie said.

Richie told Ralph the same thing he had told Potsie.

"You ought to wait a couple days," Ralph said.

"Why a couple days?"

"If Fonzie kills you today, your funeral will be on the weekend," Ralph told him. "But if you wait a couple days, it'll be on Monday or Tuesday. That way, the rest of us will get a day off from school to attend. Think of your friends."

"He isn't going to kill me."

"Can you guarantee that?" Ralph asked. "I'd like to put down some bets."

The first bell rang.

"Fonzie's late," Potsie said complainingly.

"He's loose," Ralph said. "He figures nothing's going to happen until he gets there, anyway." He frowned thoughtfully. "In this case, I guess he's right."

"What's keeping him?" Richie said. "Everybody's going in. I can't stay out here much longer."

"I don't think he's going to show," Potsie said. "I think he wore himself out chasing you and he's sleeping-in this morning."

"Let's go," Ralph said to Richie. "You don't want to be late for class. It's not worth it, just to get your head busted."

"But I want to get it over with," Richie said, frustrated.

"Listen to him," Ralph said to Potsie. "All day yesterday, he did everything he could to stay out of Fonzie's way, and now he's mad because Fonzie's a couple minutes late."

"He's nuts," Potsie said.

Richie cupped an ear. "I think I hear his bike."

Ralph and Potsie listened.

"I don't hear him," Potsie said.

Ralph agreed. "Me, neither." He started toward the school building. "Come on."

Richie hesitated.

"There isn't time to get it in between now and the next bell, anyway," Potsie said.

"Yeah. . . ."

Reluctantly, Richie joined Potsie and Ralph and the three walked toward the building.

"There's a possibility we haven't thought of," Ralph said. "Maybe Fonzie is scared."

Richie looked at him incredulously. "Of me?"

"He could be scared that he might really kill you," Ralph said.

"Oh . . ."

They reached the building and entered and walked along the corridor toward Mrs. Wimper's classroom.

"Richie. . . ," another student said. "Fonzie's looking for you."

Richie halted. "Where is he!"

"I don't know," the boy said. "I saw him last night. He said he was looking for you." The boy went on.

"Close," Potsie said. "I thought for a second that this was it."

They continued toward the classroom.

"I wonder what Fonzie'll get on the test?" Potsie said.

"Zero minus," Ralph said.

"No, he'll do okay," Richie said.

"How?"

"He got the answers," Richie said. "Not from me—but he got the answers. I forgot for a while, I was so worried about him finding me. But I remember now. He got the answers."

"Who from? Polly?"

"Polly?" Potsie said. "Polly thinks the Battle of the Bulge was a reducing diet."

"Not Polly," Richie said. "But he got the answers."

They reached the classroom just as the second bell sounded.

"That was close, boys," Mrs. Wimper told them, as they moved down the aisles toward their seats.

"We were discussing the Battle of the Bulge and didn't notice the time," Potsie told her.

She was pleased. "Well . . . as long as you were thinking about history. . . ."

Richie, Potsie and Ralph settled in their seats.

"I have your test papers," Mrs. Wimper announced. "And, first, I want to tell you how pleased I am with the results. All in all, you did extremely well."

There was a murmur of general relief.

"I'm going to pass your papers to you," Mrs. Wimper said, rising from her desk. "After that, we'll go over the questions and discuss the ones that some of you answered incorrectly."

The classroom door opened and Fonzie entered.

"Late," Mrs. Wimper told him.

"I was held up saving a lot of people from a burning building," he told her.

She waggled a finger at him. "Fonzie. . . ."

He tried again. "I had to detour to get around a herd of wild elephants on Main Street," he said.

"I'm not going to send you down to the office this time," Mrs. Wimper told him. "And I have a very special reason. I'm particularly proud of you."

"You liked that one about the elephants, huh?" Fonzie said.

"No. I'm talking about your test paper." She motioned. "If you'll take your seat, I have an announcement to make."

Fonzie headed down the aisle. "Where you been?" he said to Richie, as he approached his seat. "I been looking all over for you."

Richie swallowed. "Around," he replied.

"I want to see you," Fonzie told him.

"So I hear."

"Please, Fonzie. . . ," Mrs. Wimper said.

He sat down. "Shoot," he said to the teacher.

"My announcement concerns Fonzie—as you may have guessed," Mrs. Wimper said, addressing the class. "We're all aware, I'm sure, how difficult this has been for him, coming back to school after . . . after his long absence. . . . Well, I'm happy to tell you that he has evidently made the transition."

Blank stares.

"She means I done good," Fonzie told the class.

His classmates called out congratulations.

Richie, however, remained silent.

"Yes, Fonzie passed the test with flying colors," Mrs. Wimper said. She held up his paper. "B-plus," she announced.

Applause.

"Hey! How come I didn't get an A?" Fonzie said, protesting.

"You missed one of the questions, Fonzie."

"It must have been a trick question," he said. "Trick questions don't count. I got an A."

Mrs. Wimper sighed. "Well . . . however you want to think of it. . . ."

Fonzie rose. He pointed a finger at Richie. "I'll see you at lunch time," he told him. Then he headed for the door.

Mrs. Wimper peered at him. "Fonzie . . . where are you going?"

"To the office."

"Oh . . . did the principal—"

"He don't know it yet, but he did," Fonzie replied.

Then he was gone.

"Well, I suppose. . . ," Mrs. Wimper said dimly. Then she shrugged and began passing out the papers.

Potsie whispered to Richie. "Now, you can relax," he said. "You know exactly when you're going to get it. Noon. Twelve o'clock on the dot."

"I don't care," Richie said sadly.

"What's the matter? You were looking forward to it before."

"He took that grade and didn't say a thing about it," Richie said.

"Sure he said something. He said it should have been an A." Potsie shook his head in awe. "That's guts," he said. "Cheat on a test and then complain because you only get a B-plus. You got to admire him for his guts, Richie."

"I guess so. . . ," Richie said sorrowfully.

"Boys . . . shh-shh-shh!" Mrs. Wimper said.

At noon, Richie, Potsie and Ralph met at the school doors. Looking out, they could see Fonzie seated on his motorcycle, which was parked at the curb.

"Is that cool?" Potsie said. "He's reading a magazine. There's a guy that's about to commit mayhem and he's acting like it's nothing."

"He wouldn't be so cool if he was me," Richie said.

"When we go out, limp," Ralph said to him.

"What?"

"Limp. Like you got a bad leg," Ralph said. "Maybe he'll take pity on you."

"And try to look sick," Potsie suggested. "Fonzie wouldn't hit a sick guy."

"I don't have to look sick—I *am* sick," Richie said.

"But you don't *look* sick. Let your tongue hang out."

Richie shook his head. "Let's just get it over with," he said. "You two know what you're going to do?"

"Yeah, stand behind you and catch you when Fonzie hits you," Ralph said.

"Right. I don't want to get hurt when I fall."

"In the condition you'll be in, you probably won't notice a little hurt from a fall," Potsie said.

"Catch me, anyway."

"Okay."

"Let's go," Richie said.

They left the school building, Richie in the lead and Potsie and Ralph a step behind him, and walked toward the street.

"Dum-de-dum-dum," Potsie said.

Ahead, Fonzie raised his eyes from *Hot Rod* magazine.

"This is dumb," Richie said, halting. "Let's make a run for it."

"He'd be on us in a second with that motorcycle," Ralph pointed out.

Richie took in a deep breath and let it out slowly, then proceeded, followed once more by Potsie and Ralph.

Fonzie stuffed the magazine into his saddlebag.

"He's going to hit you with *both* fists," Potsie said to Richie.

Fonzie raised a foot to the handlebars and began tying a shoe string.

"And stomp on you," Ralph said.

When the three were almost upon him, Fonzie reached into the saddlebag and got out the book that was wrapped in plain brown paper.

"And club you," Ralph said.

"Hey!" Fonzie said amiably.

Richie halted. Ralph and Potsie stopped behind him.

"There's just one thing," Richie said to Fonzie. "Could we go over on the grass?"

"What for?"

"So when you hit me, I'll have something soft to fall on," Richie explained.

"Why would I punch you?" Fonzie asked.

Richie looked at him warily. "You're not going to?"

"Why would I?"

"Because I didn't help you cheat."

"Ahhh . . . I didn't think you would," Fonzie said. "Guys like you and Pat Boone and Dick Clark, you're too square to cheat. I never should have asked you, anyway. Cheating is something you have to do on your own. It ain't no challenge if you get help."

Richie grinned. "You're not going to hit me!"

"We came out here for nothing," Ralph complained to Potsie.

"Yeah—think it over, Fonzie," Potsie said. "Richie double-crossed you, don't forget."

"He did me a favor," Fonzie said. "I passed the test and I didn't need no help. It's a good feeling."

"Fonzie—" Richie began.

"Let me tell you why I been chasing you all over town," Fonzie said, breaking in. "I wanted to tell you thanks for, you know, getting me back in school. And, also, to tell you that I'd decided to drop out again."

"You're quitting?" Potsie said.

"That's what I said, didn't I?"

"But you've got it licked," Ralph said. "You got a B-plus."

"Yeah, I can handle that part of it," Fonzie said. "And the chicks are great, most of them, and the kids are okay, most of them, but—I don't know . . . I'm not cut out for it. Sitting in class, what I was thinking about wasn't what was going on there, but what was happening at the shop. You know, tearing an engine down, putting it back together . . . like that. . . ."

"I think about a lot of other things in class besides what's going on, too," Ralph said. "Not about engines, though."

"So," Fonzie went on, "when I left history this morning to go down to the principal's office, that's what I did. I called it off. I dropped back out."

"Why didn't you do it before?" Richie asked. "Why did you wait for the test?"

"I had to prove something."

"That you could cheat?" Richie said.

"Nah, that I could pass. I didn't want anybody to think I dropped out because I was dumb. I want them to know I did it because I'm cool."

"Fonzie, you're just fooling yourself," Richie said. "You didn't pass that test. You cheated."

Potsie addressed Ralph. "He was ahead and he couldn't keep his mouth shut," he said. "Now, Fonzie's really going to kill him."

"What cheat?" Fonzie said to Richie. "I passed that test fair and square."

"Come on, Fonzie. I saw Freeman give you the answers."

"Freeman?"

"That piece of paper he gave you," Richie said.

"That? You think that was the answers?"

"What was it if it wasn't?"

Fonzie reached into his pocket and got out a fold of paper. "This?" he said to Richie.

"Yeah, that looks like it."

Fonzie handed the paper to Richie. "Look for yourself."

Richie opened the folds. There was a drawing on the paper. "What is it, a code?" he asked.

"That's a drawing of a Stirling engine," Fonzie told him. "Wild, isn't it? No valves. Me and Freeman are building one down at the shop. It ain't going to work—I know that. I mean, with no valves. But, we're going to give it a try, anyway."

Richie handed the drawing back to him. "But, if Freeman didn't give you the answers, how did you pass the test?" he asked.

"What's the difference? I passed it."

"It does make a difference," Richie told him. "If you cheated, you didn't really pass it. You haven't proved anything, Fonzie."

"I didn't cheat."

"Then how did you do it?"

"Let's just drop it, okay?" Fonzie said.

"You cheated," Richie said.

"I believe you, Fonzie," Potsie said. "You didn't cheat."

"There, you see?" Fonzie said to Richie.

"How did you pass, then?" Richie persisted.

"Richie, take nothing for an answer, will you?" Ralph said. "Do you want to get punched?"

"I'm doing this for Fonzie's sake," Richie replied. "What good is it going to do him to go through life thinking he proved something when he didn't?"

"What good is it going to do you to go through life with a busted face?" Ralph countered.

"Okay, okay—" Fonzie broke in. "You want to know how I did it, I'll tell you." He looked around to make sure that no one was eavesdropping.

"But you got to promise me that you won't let it get any farther."

"Scout's honor," Ralph said.

Fonzie folded a hand into a fist. "Anybody that talks—"

"We promise," Richie told him. "Now, if you didn't cheat, how did you do it?"

Fonzie spoke softly. "I studied."

They stared at him in disbelief.

Ralph started to grin.

Fonzie glared.

Ralph's burgeoning grin wilted. "I believe it," he said. "You studied."

"I *did!*" Fonzie insisted.

"Okay, let's just drop the whole thing," Richie said.

"That suits me," Fonzie handed the paper-wrapped book to Potsie. "You said you wanted this," he said.

"Hey! Thanks!"

"Maybe you'll learn something from it," Fonzie said.

"Yeah, man!"

"I got to get to work," Fonzie said. "I'll see you guys at the drive-in . . . . or around or someplace." He started the engine of the motorcycle. "Keep your noses clean."

The motorcycle roared away.

"What're you looking so down-in-the-mouth about?" Potsie said to Richie. "You're alive."

"Yeah. . . ."

"So he wouldn't tell us how he cheated," Ralph

said. "We're better off not knowing. This way, we can't tell anybody and get our heads pushed in."

"I just wish he hadn't said he passed the test by studying," Richie said.

They walked back toward the school building.

"Where are we going to meet to look at this book?" Potsie said.

"A basement is the best place," Ralph told him. "Have you seen what's in it yet?"

Potsie shook his head. "Fonzie had it hidden behind *Hot Rod* magazine," he said. "I couldn't see."

"Let's take a peek."

"On school property?"

"One peek won't hurt, will it?"

"Okay."

They halted.

His hands trembling with anticipation, Potsie opened the book a crack. He scowled.

"What's the matter?" Ralph said.

Potsie opened the book wide. "It's the history text," he said, demolished.

Richie snatched the book from him. "It is!" he said, grinning. "This is what he's been hiding behind *Hot Rod* magazine! He was studying! He really did it! He passed the test by studying!"

"Talk about a dirty trick!" Potsie said. "A history text!"

"But if he passed the test by studying," Ralph said to Richie, "why doesn't he want anybody to know?"

"It's not cool," Richie explained. "Studying's not cool."

"Oh."

"Everybody will think he cheated—just like we did," Richie said.

Ralph nodded. "The only thing is," he said, "if he has everybody thinking he cheated—but he really studied—isn't that cheating?"

Richie considered for a moment. "I'll have to ask my father," he said. "He understands questions like that."

When Richie asked his father the question at dinner that evening, Howard came back instantly with an answer.

"Yes and no," he said.

"I guess it doesn't make that much difference," Richie said, piling green beans onto his plate.

"Richie, you don't like green beans," his mother reminded him.

"I missed lunch today," he explained, "even green beans look good to me."

"You shouldn't skip lunch."

"I was talking to Fonzie, getting things straightened out."

"Can we assume that he didn't kill you?" Howard asked.

"He wasn't even mad," Richie replied. "We're still friends." He poured gravy onto his mashed potatoes. "He dropped out of school again," he added.

"Oh . . . that's a shame," Marion said. "Now, he won't be able to be a policeman."

"Somehow, I think I'll sleep better, knowing that," Howard said.

"He's going to stick to being a mechanic," Richie said. "It's what he likes."

"That's very important," Howard said. "And, mechanics are important, too. We have all of these wonderful modern conveniences, cars, television sets, washing machines. . . . But, without mechanics and repairmen they wouldn't be much good. They're machines. And machines break down. If there weren't someone to fix them, there wouldn't be much point to inventing them in the first place."

"And Fonzie's a great mechanic, too," Richie said.

"That helps. There's a lot of satisfaction in being really good at something. And, there's a lot of unhappiness in doing something you don't really like to do just for the money or the prestige."

"Fonzie's building an engine without valves," Richie said.

"Without valves?"

Richie nodded.

"Is there a valve shortage?" Howard asked.

"No, it's supposed to not have valves."

"What does it have instead?"

Richie thought for a moment, then shrugged. "Nothing, I guess," he said.

"Oh. Well, there's no shortage of that." Howard turned to his daughter. "And how was your day, Joanie? You didn't get killed, either, I notice."

"We had our first Junior Chipmunks meeting," she told him.

"Junior Chipmunks?"

"It's like the Girl Scouts," Marion old him.

"Oh. How did it go, Joanie?"

"Great!" she said enthusiastically. "Jennie Drysdale threw up!"

Howard looked at his food. "Maybe you can tell us about it later," he said.

"Speaking of Junior Chipmunks," Marion said, "that reminds me. I'll need the car tomorrow, Howard. I have to run some errands for the P.T.A."

"How will I get to work?" he asked.

"I'll drive you."

"Just ask her about sex and she'll drive you anywhere," Joanie told her father.

Howard drew back, staring at her. "What's that supposed to mean?"

"It means your daughter is growing up," Marion said.

Howard sighed. He was silent for a second. Then he sighed again.

"What's the matter, dear?" Marion asked.

"I was just picturing a grown-up chipmunk," he said. "She'll be needing braces for her teeth."